Carving Folk Art Figures

By Shawn Cipa

Fox Chapel Publishing Co. Inc.

1970 Broad Street • East Petersburg, PA 17520 • www.foxchapelpublishing.com

Dedication
To my family and friends, and especially to my wife, Joanne.

Acknowledgments
Thanks to Woodcraft for the opportunity to compete in their annual Santa carving contest, and to Fox Chapel Publishing for the opportunity to publish a book.

Carving Folk Art Figures is an original work, first published in 2002 by Fox Chapel Publishing Company, Inc. The patterns contained herein are copyrighted by the author. Artists may make three copies of the patterns for personal use. The patterns themselves, however, are not to be duplicated for resale or distribution under any circumstances. This is a violation of copyright law.

Publisher	Alan Giagnocavo
Project Editor	Ayleen Stellhorn
Interior Photography	Shawn Cipa
Desktop Specialist	Paul Cipa, Identity Element
Cover Design	Keren Holl

ISBN #1–56523–171–6
Library of Congress Preassigned Card Number: 2002102606

To order your copy of this book,
please send check or money order
for the cover price plus $3.00 shipping to:
Fox Books
1970 Broad Street
East Petersburg, PA 17520

Or visit us on the web at
www.foxchapelpublishing.com

Printd in China
10 9 8 7 6 5 4 3 2

Because carving wood and other materials inherently includes the risk of injury and damage, this book cannot guarantee that creating the projects in this book is safe for everyone. For this reason, this book is sold without warranties or guarantees of any kind, express or implied, and the publisher and author disclaim any liability for any injuries, losses or damages caused in any way by the content of this book or the reader's use of the tools needed to complete the projects presented here. The publisher and the author urge all carvers to thoroughly review each project and to understand the use of all tools involved before beginning any project.

Table of Contents •••••••••••••••••••••

Foreword

In the world of woodcarving there is always a need for new patterns and projects to keep all those carvers who don't draw busy. This makes a nice niche for those who draw and design. Shawn Cipa fits right into this special place with his patterns and carvings, and what better thing to do than write a book about what you do best. This volume should help populate the country with all kinds of Santas and angels. There's nothing better than sharing what you have with others, especially if it's something everyone likes. Who doesn't like carving ol' Saint Nick?

I know there are a lot of carving books on the market. Who would have thought there would be hundreds. I'm glad to see all this documented for future carvers. Right now is the golden age of woodcarving in the U.S. It's a good time for Shawn to jump right in here with his offerings. As I see it, Shawn is putting out some great material. This volume should inspire a lot of folks to get out their tools and go to work. Shawn, do you know how many happy carving hours you'll be responsible for?

—*Harold Enlow*

The Art of Whimsy

Introduction

Having developed a solid art background since I was a small child, one thing pleasantly surprised me when I was first introduced to my local woodcarving community—there are no secrets. Fellow carvers were eager to take me under their wings and show me whatever they knew, whether I asked or not. I marveled at all the books, compilations and samples that were available to me, whenever I wanted them. I was also taken back when people would start to ask *me* questions: "What's your favorite wood?" "How do you sharpen your knife?" and most surprisingly, " Can you show me how you did that?"

Eight years and many chips later, I have been given the golden opportunity to compose a book myself. Drawing, painting and sculpting in clay have always been easy for me. Woodcarving has not. It was a daunting task to master the tools, let alone keep them sharp. But I feverishly kept at it and soon became addicted to the feel and smell of the wood. Now, the only time I draw is to create a carving pattern. The only time I paint is when I am finishing a carved piece. Instead of clay, I now sculpt wood. As irony would have it, it seems all my previous abilities have only been to facilitate my true calling. I now mainly rely on my sense of composition and stylization in the creative process. Big words? Not really. All it means is to be yourself, keep it real and, above all else, enjoy what you do. It is my hope that I can impart to you some of what I have learned thus far.

As a woodcarver, I am inspired by the whimsical nature of things. Santa Claus, angels and other imaginary figures appeal most to me. Carving these types of subjects allows me a certain freedom because there are no boundaries or hard, fast rules. Santa, for example, is a mythical character. That means I can make him look anyway I choose. Everyone has his or her own particular image of what the old Elf should look like, and none of these is wrong. These types of characters spur the imagination in people, and this is the basis of an original idea.

My designs are stylized. What I mean is that instead of complete realism, I try to rely on the overall shape and color to create a mood. Sometimes just a little tilt of the head shows all the expression you need. It can give an otherwise static pose a subtle "action." The simpler patterns in this book are basic shapes to provide for easy band sawing of the rough blank. In order to bring out character in the piece, I rely less on the complexity of the shape and more on the detail carved into the surface. Depending on your skill level, you can apply as much or as little detail as you desire. Some of the other patterns in this book are more complex on varying degrees, providing a range of difficulty levels. In this manner, beginning carvers have things to encourage them while intermediate carvers also have a challenge. I also provide suggestions throughout to alter patterns. This is especially helpful in developing your own creativity, possibly leading to designing your own ideas—and that is what it is all about.

If you have no desire to strive to that level, that's okay too. Check out my patterns, carve them, and have fun. Because they will be carved by you alone, that still makes them an original, one-of-a-kind piece that will truly be something to be proud of.

—Shawn Cipa
cipa@cobweb.net

Getting Started

Wood choice

Basswood is probably the most common and popular carving wood. It holds great detail yet is soft enough to work without difficulty. Although basswood can be left natural, it is most often chosen when the carving is to be painted. This is because it contains next to no figure, or grain. This is my wood of choice in this book.

You could also choose to use white pine, which is also a great whittling wood, but it has its limitations. White pine cannot hold a great amount of detail; small pieces tend to break off easily. Nevertheless, if you like working with white pine, adjust the pattern to suit your needs.

Butternut is an excellent carving wood and is fairly soft. This type of wood will hold great detail, however, care must be taken as some pieces can be quite brittle. Butternut has a very prominently figured grain. This, combined with its rich caramel color, makes for an attractive carving if left natural. If you choose to use this wood with any of my patterns, just finish it with a clear coat.

Although there are many excellent hardwoods for carving, such as black walnut and cherry, I recommend that you avoid using them for the projects in this book. They are extremely hard to work with while using a knife and usually require a vise instead of holding the piece in your hands while carving. Other soft whittling woods that would work well for the projects in this book include tupelo, willow, poplar and jelutong.

Basswood can be found at most hardwood lumberyards. It can also be ordered from any one of the many carving supply catalogs, although this is almost always the more expensive alternative. On the upside, you get what you pay for: Carving supply stores usually carry high-quality wood. Probably the best source is to contact your local woodcarving club. If you are not a member, become one. Someone always seems to have a good, cheap source for basswood. Sometimes the wood is even free! It just goes to show how generous fellow woodcarvers can be.

Tools and sharpening

With a vast array of tools on the market, it's hard to know where to begin. Start with the basics: a good carving knife, a v-tool, and two or three half round gouges of varying sizes ($\frac{1}{16}$ inch, $\frac{1}{8}$ inch, and $\frac{1}{4}$ inch). If possible, have a good fishtail gouge on hand also. Over the years I have collected at least 70 gouges and countless knives. Is this necessary? Of course not, but there exists a specific tool that performs a specific job in any given project. It seems the more you carve, the more tools you find showing up in your toolbox. A carving can easily be completed with just a knife or two, but additional tools make certain cuts easier to perform, which speeds up your progress.

As far as most of the projects in this book are concerned, the tool requirement is minimal. My personal course of action for small projects is as follows: rough it out with a large 2-inch knife, switch to a smaller knife to clean it up, then use small palm gouges for details. There are lots of good knives on the market, but I am in the habit of making my own from either straight razor blades or good steel from old snapped-off pocketknives.

A sharp tool is essential. You'd think this goes without saying, but there are so many beginners who struggle on a piece of wood only to give up in frustration. They blame themselves, thinking they don't have what it takes, when all along a dull tool is the culprit. To carve with the sharpest of tools is a joy that must be experienced to be appreciated.

A good carving knife plus some palm tools and gouges are needed to carve the projects in this book.

Learning to successfully sharpen is an art unto itself. It's practically "half the battle" when learning to carve. It took several years to become comfortable with my own sharpening skills, and I tried many different stones and accessories. I finally bought a motorized wet grinder. I get an edge fast, but I have to be careful not to end up with a little nub for a tool. It would take a whole chapter or two to go over sharpening specifics, so I suggest purchasing a good sharpening book from your favorite local or mail order carving supply store. However, there are a few basic steps to follow when sharpening a knife:

• Using a good bench stone (I suggest a combination Japanese water stone with coarse and fine grits), remove any heel or bevel that the knife may have with the coarse grit. You want the blade to have two flat planes, like a wedge. For carving soft woods like basswood, an angle of 15 or 20 degrees is required. Notice the illustration.

• Using the fine grit, sharpen both sides equally, pushing the edge *toward* the abrasive until a small wire burr develops. Once you have the burr, you have gone as far as the stone can take you.

• Remove the wire burr by stropping. This is done by polishing the planes of the knife on a flat piece of leather charged with jeweler's rouge or a similar substance. Be sure to pull the edge *away* from the surface this time. Stroke both sides equally until the burr is completely removed. This should leave you with a nice sharp edge, ready for carving.

If you have sharpened correctly, all you need to maintain the edge is to strop often: before each carving session and every 15 or 20 minutes during carving. The key is to never let your tool become dull. Eventually the edge will round over and you will need to use the stone again. To test for sharpness, *carefully* place the edge of the knife on your fingernail and drag it lightly across. If it "sticks," the blade is sharp. If it slides across easily, you need to sharpen the blade.

Remember, a sharp knife is a safe knife. Why? If the knife is dull, you will struggle more than necessary, possibly slip and cut yourself. When the blade is nice and sharp, it should glide through the wood easily. Of course, a sharp knife will easily glide through your finger as well, so it's a good idea to use some protection. A cut-resistant glove works well and is usually worn on the hand holding the carving. In the very least, use a thumb guard or some carver's latex-coated "thumb tape." Common sense helps. Whenever possible, keep your fingers out of the path of the intended cut. Apply pressure with the thumb of the hand opposite the carving hand to improve stability. Focus; don't carve in a distracting or poorly lit atmosphere.

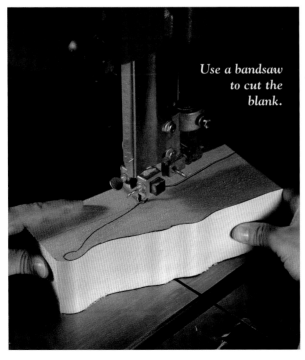

Use a bandsaw to cut the blank.

Preparing wood

You will want to photocopy the patterns from this book to use as a template. If the carvings are actually bigger than could fit on the page, I have provided the enlargement percentage to use. Of course, you could carve these figures any size you want. The sizes shown here make it easy to hold the figure while carving.

Just cut out the pattern and trace it onto the block of wood you have prepared, making sure that the front and side are lined up. Also, be sure to lay out the pattern lengthwise with the grain. I have marked the dimensions required for each pattern.

You can then proceed to cut out the shape using a band saw or a coping saw. A few words about coping saws. Unless you are a purist and are proficient with the use of a coping saw, don't bother. I have found coping saws very difficult to use, and it can get frustrating when the saws drift off course. The simpler patterns are extremely easy to band saw. Some of the others get a little more involved.

If you can, saw the front pattern first and leave the scrap sides whole. Then take masking tape and put the pieces back in place to "re-form" the whole block. This way, you can then saw the side pattern with stability. Remember to saw outside the lines, leaving about a $^1/_{16}$-inch margin. This gives you a little play.

One last tip when sawing: It saves a lot of time to knock off the hard corners wherever possible. To do this, tilt your band saw table to 45 degrees and carefully shave off the hard edges. Be careful not to pinch the blade during this procedure.

Basic knife cuts

Some of the basic knife cuts I use in this book are as follows:
•Stop cut. This is usually a plunge cut made with the tip of knife directly into the surface. Wood is then removed up to that plunge cut, effectively stopping the knife from going any further. I use this cut to separate main shapes from each other.
•Chip cut. This is a sort of triangular geometric cut. The knife tip is plunged in on an angle, three times (like a triangle), with the deepest part meeting together. The result is a three-sided chip popping out, leaving a matching hole. I use this cut to separate intersecting areas.
•Scallop cuts. This cut is used to hollow out an area, to make it slightly concave. Lightly pare away the wood in the desired area, biting in and fluidly pulling out with a turn of the wrist. Take small bites, otherwise you may mar the burnished surface that the knife should leave.

Painting and finishing

Every carver seems to have his own painting and finishing techniques that he swears by. I have tried several that I like and dislike. Eventually personal experimentation leads to the method that suits you best. The method I will describe has been applied to all the carvings shown in this book.

I use acrylic paints as opposed to oils because they dry faster and they are easier to clean up. The cheap craft types in the one-ounce plastic bottles are great to use. They are inexpensive, good quality and have a huge variety of colors to choose from, which virtually eliminates the need to mix colors. Acrylics dry very fast (five to six minutes) and matte, not glossy.

A variety of paintbrushes are needed to paint the projects in this book.

Since you won't be spending much on paint, invest in good brushes. Really cheap ones are very hard to work with, and they fall apart. I would suggest a high-quality synthetic or sable brush. You will want at least three sizes: a $1/2$-inch flat brush for blocking in colors, a $1/4$-inch round brush for getting into corners and some detailing, and a very small round brush for detailing. Make sure to always clean your brushes well after each use, especially when using acrylics.

When applying the paint to the wood, do not use the paint at full strength. One choice is to dip the brush in water before dipping it in the paint. A second choice is to mix up a little wash of acrylic paint and water on a palette (baby jar lid) before applying. I personally do not like my paints too washed out, as some carvers do. Don't be afraid to put it on strong, just be sure to temper it with a little water. This also helps the paint to flow onto the wood as it is often rather thick.

When using white, off-white or yellow acrylics, I like to put the paint on almost full strength or use several coats of a thinner wash. When using a metallic paint like gold or silver, use it at full strength. If you don't, the "shimmery" effect will be lost. You'll also find that after acrylics dry, they will have a harsh, chalky look. This is okay; we'll take care of that next.

After the paint has dried for at least an hour, seal the carving with a high quality, fast-drying satin polyurethane. Make sure you use satin, not gloss! It is important that you apply this finish as thin as possible. I practically scrub it on with a disposable stain brush, working it into all the crevices. This will maintain the matte quality when the finish dries. This step is done for two reasons: to brighten up the colors and, more importantly, to seal the carving for antiquing. If you skip this step and try to antique the carving without sealing first, you will end up with a big mess.

Let the carving dry overnight. When dry, the piece should still look matte. A dull sheen is okay. I like to antique my carvings. It pulls out the details and softens the pieces. To achieve this, I use an oil-based gel wood stain. Oil-based gel is good for two reasons. First, if your polyurethane got a little too thick somewhere and left a shine, the stain will help to dull that area a bit. Secondly, gel doesn't run. Whenever you use stain—gel or liquid—there is always some excess left in the nooks and crannies. When left to dry, liquid stain will eventually run out a bit and leave a little brown run mark. Gel stays put.

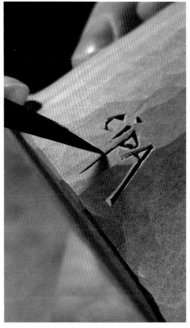

The color of the stain is up to you. I prefer to use anything titled "antique oak," "colonial" or "old oak." These colors appear to be dark brown, but leave a warm, almost yellowed effect. Sometimes "fruitwood" is nice if you want an even more subtle effect.

Apply the stain with another disposable brush, working it into the deeper details. Slather it on! Then wipe it all off with a cotton rag. Make sure you do this immediately, as gel stain dries quickly. You want the effect to be subtle. If you leave the gel on more than a minute, you will have a hard time getting it back off. Let the wiped-off carving dry overnight, and your carving is complete.

Be sure to dispose of your oily rags properly after use. Consult the safety precautions on the labels of your products. Don't forget to sign your carvings. Use a permanent ink pen, a burning tool or a v-tool.

This guy makes a great beginning project. I have chosen him as the first demonstration piece because many of the skills you'll need to carve the rest of the pieces in this book are addressed as you carve this Old World Santa. He also has a very basic shape, which makes it easy to rough out with the band saw.

You will learn basic carving techniques such as whittling, stop cutting and chip cutting plus how to use gouges to create texture. You will also learn how to paint and finish your carving, bringing it to life through color. Remember that the colors I choose are a guide; feel free to come up with your own color scheme. If you are already familiar with these techniques, sit back and enjoy an easy piece that is fun to carve. It will take your mind off that detailed masterpiece that you may be working on.

Once you have completed this Santa, take a look at the Ideas Page I have provided. Try another Santa, this time changing his features. This is designed to help you create your own ideas, which will make your piece truly an original. Take your time; don't try to finish this carving all in one sitting. Sometimes you lose your perspective if you rush through. Most of all, have fun!

Materials List: Carving

- Basswood block 3" x 2.5" x 10"
- Larger bladed rough-out knife
- Smaller bladed detail knife
- 1/2" fish tail gouge with a #12 sweep (optional)
- #12 1/4" v-tool
- 1/8" veiner gouge (half-round)
- Pencil or fine marker
- Band saw
- Carving glove or thumb tape for protection

Materials List: Painting and Finishing

- 1/2" flat brush for large areas
- 1/4" round brush for smaller areas
- 1/8" round brush
- Very fine detail brush
- Barn red
- Forest green
- Titanium white
- Antique white
- Flesh tone
- Bright red
- Leaf green
- Bright yellow
- Mauve
- Deep purple
- Gold
- Fast drying satin polyurethane
- Brown gel wood stain
- Disposable stain brush
- Cotton rag

Old World Santa

This pattern is a great beginning project,
with a simple shape and room for detail.
I have carved this guy hundreds of times in various
versions. He is probably the first Santa pattern
I ever designed, stemming from the fact that
I only had small, narrow scraps of wood to carve
when I first started. Your beginning block before
sawing will need to measure 3" x 2$\frac{1}{2}$" x 10".
My personal color choices are mentioned in the
demonstration. Once you have completed the
carving, try another one: This time make some
changes like the ones I show on the "Ideas" page.

Pattern on page 10.

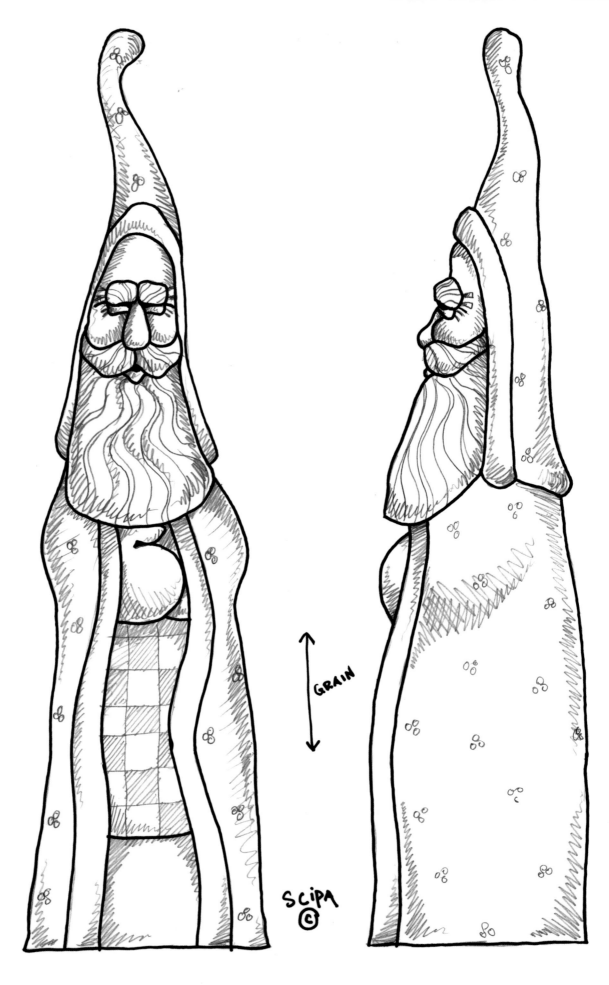

GRAIN

SCIPA ©

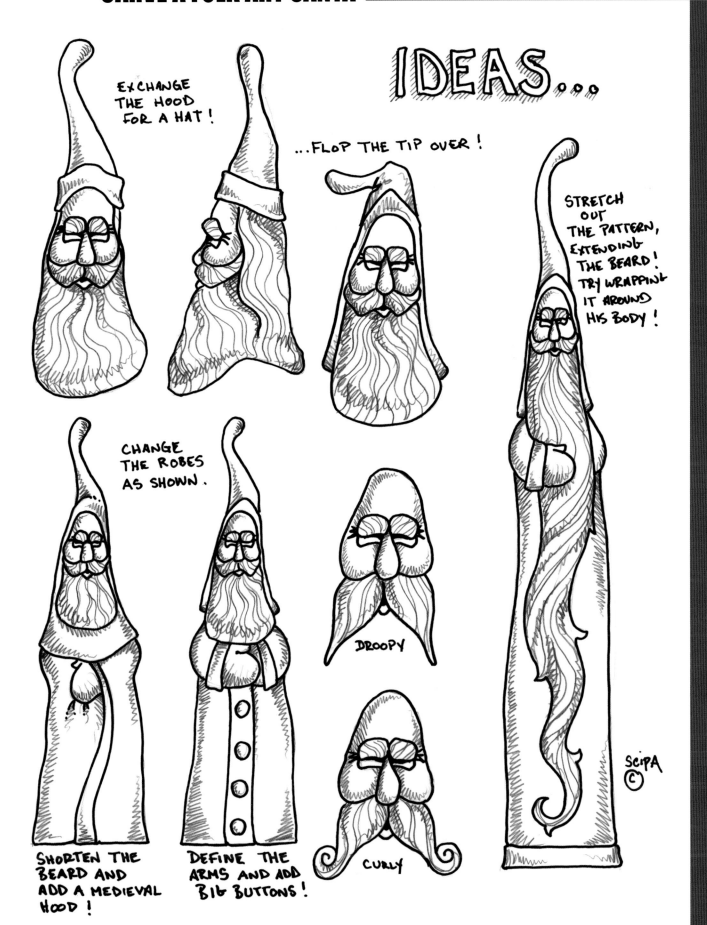

IDEAS...

EXCHANGE THE HOOD FOR A HAT!

...FLOP THE TIP OVER!

STRETCH OUT THE PATTERN, EXTENDING THE BEARD! TRY WRAPPING IT AROUND HIS BODY!

CHANGE THE ROBES AS SHOWN.

DROOPY

SHORTEN THE BEARD AND ADD A MEDIEVAL HOOD!

DEFINE THE ARMS AND ADD BIG BUTTONS!

CURLY

SCIPA ©

Read the section "Preparing wood" in Chapter One. Using the pattern on page 10 as a template, bandsaw the blank. The prepared blank should look like this. Shown is the front view.

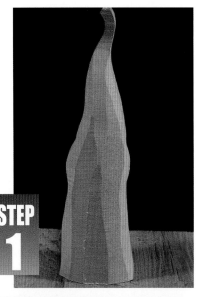

STEP 1

Here is the side view. Notice how I have shaved the corners with the band saw.

STEP 2

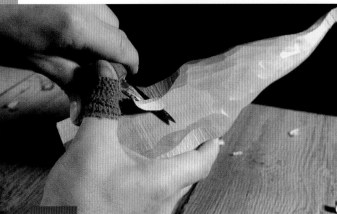

STEP 3

Using my larger rough-out knife, I first knock off the corners and round out the entire body, making sure not to alter the general contour. This first step helps to "erase" all the saw marks.

STEP 4

Be sure not to carve away the arm "bulges" on each side.

STEP 5

Carefully round the tip of Santa's hood into a knob.

STEP 6

Smooth out the body. Notice the simple shape of the carving—ready for details already.

STEP 7

Using a marker or pencil, draw a line separating the head from the rest of the body. The front and the back should be about the same height. On the sides, swoop the line up to suggest shoulders. Refer to the pattern for line placement.

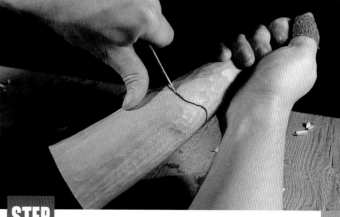

STEP 8

With the knife, plunge along the line to make a stop cut. Go all the way around the carving.

STEP 9

Use the knife to taper the body up to the stop cut. This will make the head stand out. You may have to go back and deepen the stop cut a little. Work all the way around, going about a ⅛ inch deep. This step further defines the arm bulges.

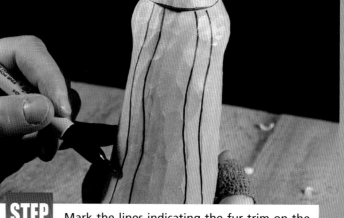

STEP 10

Mark the lines indicating the fur trim on the coat. Make them wavy instead of straight to provide some character. Be sure to leave enough space for the gloves—about ¾ inch.

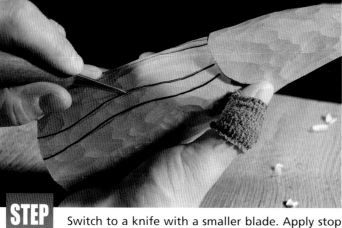
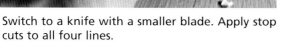

STEP 11

Switch to a knife with a smaller blade. Apply stop cuts to all four lines.

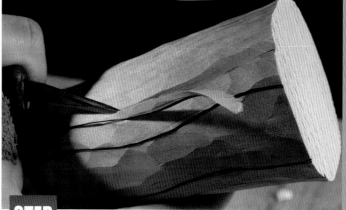

STEP 12

Carve away wood to define the outer edge of the fur trim, but don't carve too deep. Do both sides.

STEP 13 With the knife, clear away a portion of the wood on the inside of the fur trim. Go about a 1/8-inch deep.

STEP 14 Draw in the gloves, referring to the pattern. Only one glove fully shows, with just a hint of the other underneath.

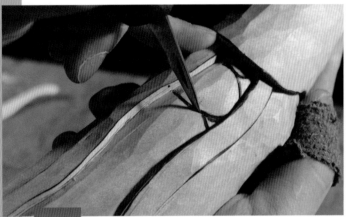

STEP 15 Make a stop cut along the lines. Don't forget the tiny portion of the other glove underneath.

STEP 16 With the knife, remove wood from below the gloves to define them. Taper up from the bottom, working down to about 1/4 inch deep at the glove.

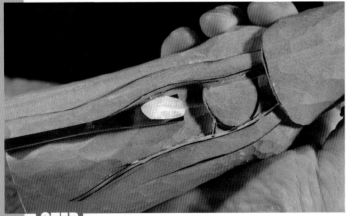

STEP 17 A small fishtail gouge can be helpful for tapering this area, especially when getting into the crevices. I'm using a #12 sweep here.

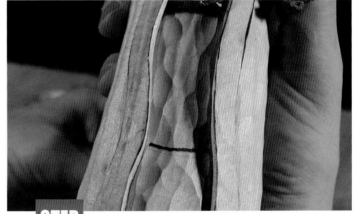

STEP 18 Draw in the hem of the inner robe.

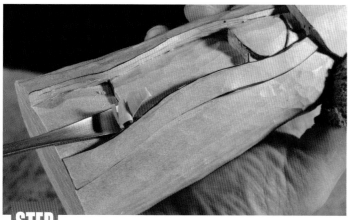

STEP 19
Make a stop cut and taper up from the bottom to suggest overlapping robes.

STEP 20
Using the knife, carefully remove wood from around the outer glove, separating it from the one underneath. Don't carve too deep! Be careful not to chip out around the thumb.

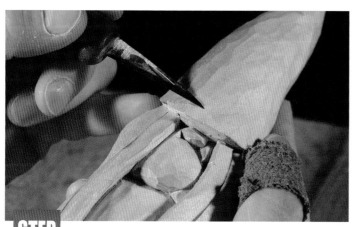

STEP 21
Using the knife, round out the glove and define the thumb using a series of chip cuts.

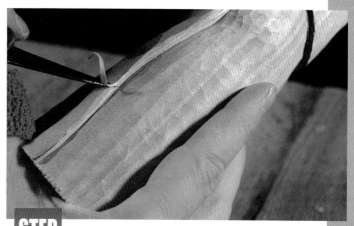

STEP 22
Round off the hard edges on the fur trim.

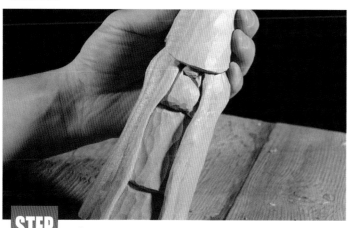

STEP 23
Clean up any rough areas, round off hard edges, and the body is complete. Now for the head! This is a good time to strop your knife.

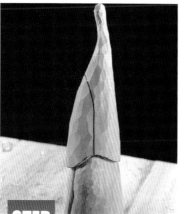

STEP 24
Draw a line separating the hood from the facial area, starting on the side at the high point of the shoulders. Also, mark the center of the face.

STEP 25 Make a stop cut along the line.

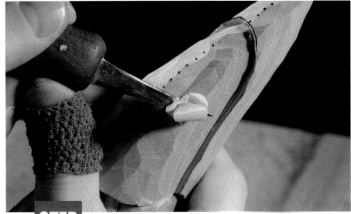

STEP 26 Using the knife, remove wood from the face and beard area to define the edge of the hood. Make the hood appear to be about 1/8-inch thick.

STEP 27 Narrow the face a bit, tapering toward the center line as shown by the arrows.

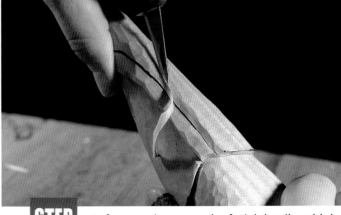

STEP 28 Before moving on to the facial details, add the fur trim around the edge of the hood. Draw in the line, make a stop cut, and slice away just enough to define the trim. Don't forget to round off the hard edge.

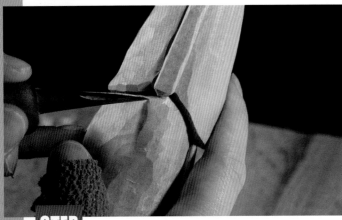

STEP 29 I like to make two little chip cuts, one at the bottom edge of the beard and hood, and one at the bottom edge of the trim and hood.

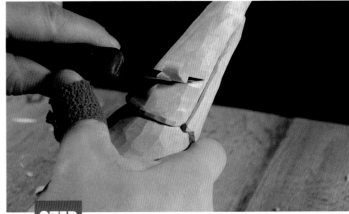

STEP 30 Next, use the knife to thin out the back of the hood a little. Scallop out the bottom edge, which gives the hood more form.

CARVE A FOLK ART SANTA STEP BY STEP

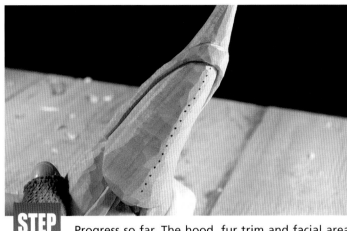

STEP 31
Progress so far. The hood, fur trim and facial area are re-formed.

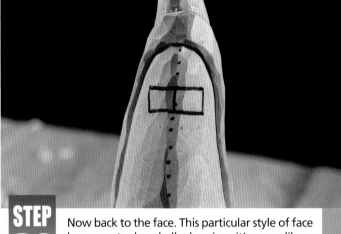

STEP 32
Now back to the face. This particular style of face has no actual eyeballs showing; it's more like a "squint." It's a more simplistic, yet effective way to enhance the "jolly" smile. Start with the eyebrows, drawing them in as rectangles.

STEP 33
With the knife, make a stop cut on the bottom line of the eyebrows. About half an inch below that, cut out a wedge up to the brow. As you can see, this starts to define the profile of the nose.

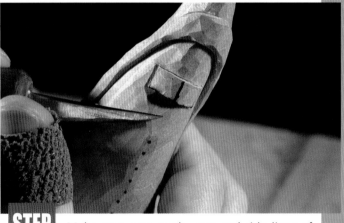

STEP 34
Make stop cuts on the top and side lines of the brow. Remove a very small wedge of wood around it, and blend the brow back into the forehead and temples.

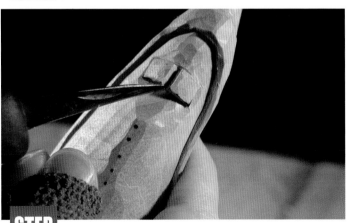

STEP 35
Separate the brows by removing a small wedge through the center.

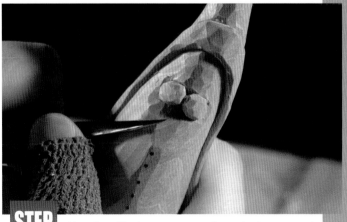

STEP 36
Knock off the corners of each brow and round the edges, as shown.

Carving Folk Art Figures 17

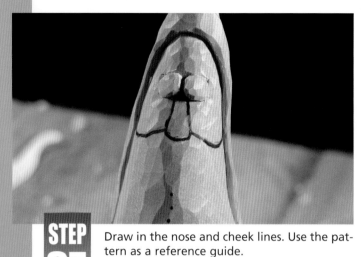

STEP 37
Draw in the nose and cheek lines. Use the pattern as a reference guide.

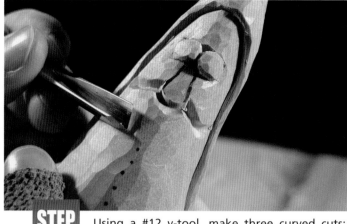

STEP 38
Using a #12 v-tool, make three curved cuts: one for each cheek and one for the nose. This separates the face from the mustache and beard.

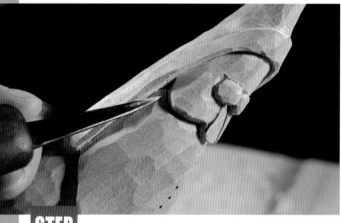

STEP 39
Using the knife, clean up the v-cuts by tapering the mustache area. Define the cheeks and the nose ball.

STEP 40
Make stop cuts to separate the nose from the cheeks. Try to plunge clean and deep on the first pass.

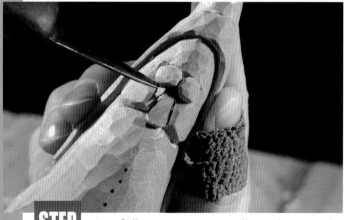

STEP 41
Carefully remove a small wedge at the cheek/nose line. Carry this wedge through up to the brow. Do both sides.

STEP 42
Progress so far. With all the main facial features defined, use the knife to clean up the face by rounding the cheeks and the nose. Slightly hollow the temples, reshaping the face.

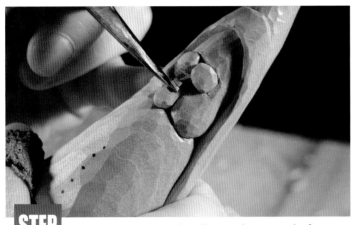

STEP 43

Next, two minor details on the nose before we move on to the eyes. I like to scallop out a tiny amount of wood midway up the nose to give some character. It gives the figure a little bony bump on the nose bridge.

STEP 44

Create nostrils by scooping out a tiny amount in the appropriate area.

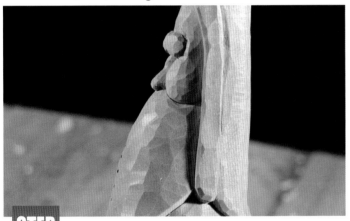

STEP 45

A profile of the face. Notice the nose bridge and the character that the slight bump created.

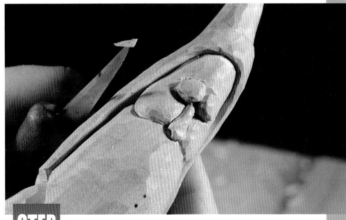

STEP 46

Remove a tiny sliver of wood right under the brow to make a "squint." Don't remove too much or it will look like an empty eye socket.

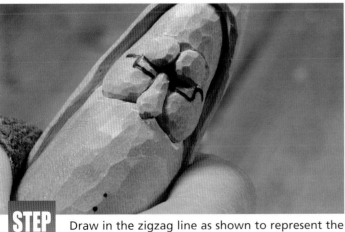

STEP 47

Draw in the zigzag line as shown to represent the bags under the eyes.

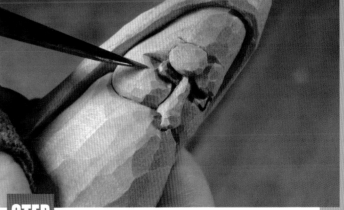

STEP 48

Make three stop cuts on these lines and carefully remove a small amount from underneath, tapering up from the cheek. Watch that you don't chip out the eye bag. Do both sides.

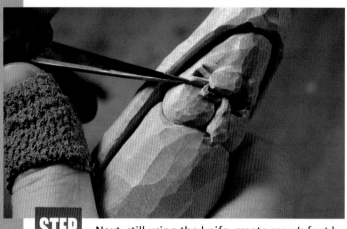

STEP 49 Next, still using the knife, create crow's feet by applying small chip cuts in the temple area as shown. Two on each side is good.

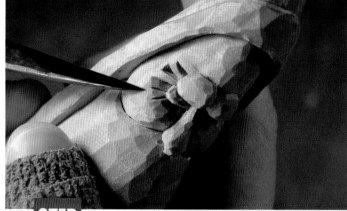

STEP 50 One more eye detail. I like to add two little wrinkles coming out from under the eye bag. Do this by creating little v-cuts with the knife. If this step seems excessive to you, don't worry. It will all pop out when we paint and antique.

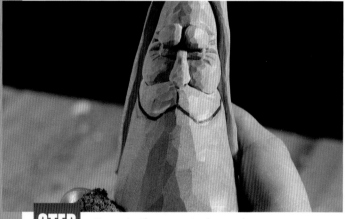

STEP 51 Draw in the moustache as shown.

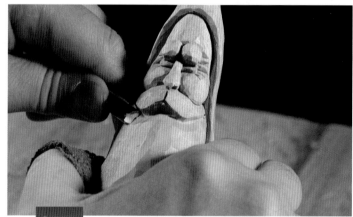

STEP 52 Using the #12 v-tool, define the mustache.

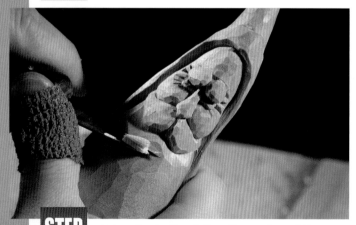

STEP 53 Using the knife, define the center of the mustache. Taper the beard and round off the edges.

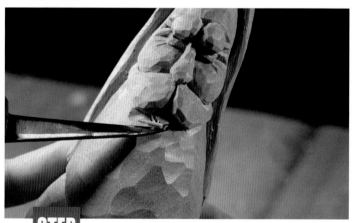

STEP 54 Draw in the lower lip. Using stop cuts, remove wood under the lip to define it. Taper up from the beard.

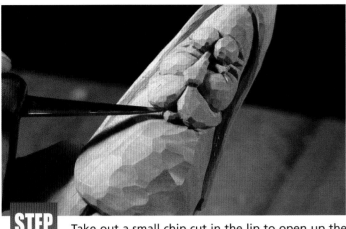

STEP 55

Take out a small chip cut in the lip to open up the mouth. Also, round off the lip.

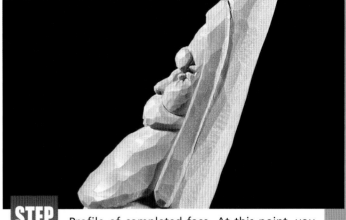

STEP 56

Profile of completed face. At this point, you could stop. However, if you wish to texture the beard and the fur trim, I've added a few more steps.

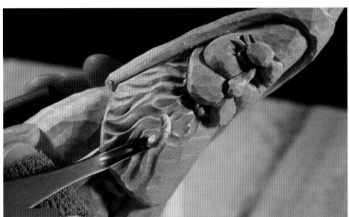

STEP 57

To texture the beard, I use a small 1/8-inch veiner gouge. Apply as much texture as you like, remembering not to carve straight lines. It's important to let the lines intersect one another. I like to make mine especially wavy.

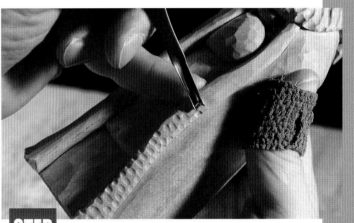

STEP 58

To texture the fur trim on the coat and hood, use the same veiner gouge. Cut small, shallow scoops very close together.

STEP 59

Your carving is complete, ready for painting.

A side view of the carved piece.

STEP 60

STEP 1

Before painting, lightly clean the carving with a mild dishwashing soap and a toothbrush. This helps to remove oils from your hands. After it has dried, pencil in a few light guidelines on Santa's inner robe.

STEP 2

Starting with the coat and hood, apply barn red with a large flat brush. Actually, any red will do; I prefer to stay away from the real bright ones, such as fire engine red. A burgundy or maroon is a nice alternative.

STEP 3

Using a smaller round brush, apply forest green for the gloves.

STEP 4

For the beard, I prefer to use an antique white, saving the true white for the fur trim. Apply the whites a little thicker than the other colors. Use the small brush for the brows and mustache, and the larger one for the beard.

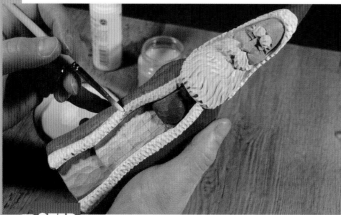

STEP 5

Using the small round brush, paint the fur trim titanium (true) white.

STEP 6

Using the small round brush, paint the face a flesh tone.

STEP 7

Blending a little bright red with the flesh tone helps to give the cheeks a rosy glow. Apply a little of this blend to the cheek and blend it back. Add some to the tip of the nose as well. Paint the lips with this mixture, too.

STEP 8

Use a bright leaf green for half of the checker pattern on the inner robe. Paint every other one with an extra-small round brush. Use bright yellow for the remaining checkered squares.

STEP 9

Paint the bottom skirt with mauve. For depth, blend a little deep purple with the mauve to shade the area around the overlap of the robes, as shown here.

STEP 10

As a final touch, add a little dot pattern in full-strength gold to the coat and hood. Use the extra-small round brush. Let the carving dry for at least an hour.

STEP 11

Next seal the carving with satin polyurethane. Apply the coat as thin as you possibly can with a cheap stain brush, scrubbing it into the nooks. Watch the colors pop out as you do this! It will go on shiny, but if you put it on thin, it will dry almost matte. Let the carving dry overnight.

STEP 12

Using the same brush, apply a brown gel wood stain. Slather it on, working it into the nooks. Immediately wipe off the excess with a clean cotton rag. Let the carving dry overnight before handling it.

This Angel makes an excellent second demonstration because she builds on the skills that were addressed in the Santa demonstration. Her body is still very simply shaped, but the face is a little more difficult. These techniques will help you accomplish the other Angel patterns in this book. Because of the wings and halo, this piece will require some simple assembly skills. This helps to prepare you for some other similar tasks required in some of the other patterns.

You may choose to use your own color scheme for your angel. For example, I like to use a green theme with my red heads. Blondes look good in blue or purple, and brunettes look good in red. Everyone looks good in white and gold!

Once again, consult the Ideas page I have provided with this pattern. Use these variations to help spur your own additions to your carving. Use a different hairstyle or a different wing pattern to create an Angel that is uniquely your own.

Materials List: Carving

- Basswood block
- Two basswood pieces, each 5" x 2" x ³/₈" thick
- Larger bladed rough-out knife
- Smaller bladed detail knife
- #12 ¼" v-tool
- ¹/₈" veiner gouge (half-round)
- ¹/₁₆" veiner gouge (half-round)
- ¼" shallow gouge
- Pencil or fine marker
- Soft craft wire, thin gauge
- Small pliers
- Small ¹/₂" wire nails
- Yellow wood glue
- Instant crazy glue
- Hand drill with ¹/₁₆" bit
- Band saw
- Carving glove or thumb tape for protection

Materials List: Painting and Finishing

- ¹/₂" flat brush for large areas
- ¼" round brush for smaller areas
- ¹/₈" round brush
- Very fine detail brush
- Olive green
- Titanium white
- Antique white
- Sage green
- Mint green
- Flesh tone
- Bright red
- Cinnamon
- Tangerine orange
- Gold
- Fast drying satin polyurethane
- Brown gel wood stain
- Disposable stain brush
- Cotton rag

Angel

This angel is nice and simple. I have designed a face that is easy to accomplish for beginning and intermediate carvers alike. The features are minimal, but the face still retains a female expression. Your block will need to measure 3" x 3" x 10". I have provided step-by-step instructions for carving the wings separately and attaching them.

By carving the wings separately, the overall carving will be much stronger than if carved from a single piece of wood.

The stock for the wings should be 5" x 2" x ³/₈". If you wish, mix and match the other wing patterns found in this book for a different look. Don't forget to attach the halo when all else is done!

Pattern on pages 26 and 27.

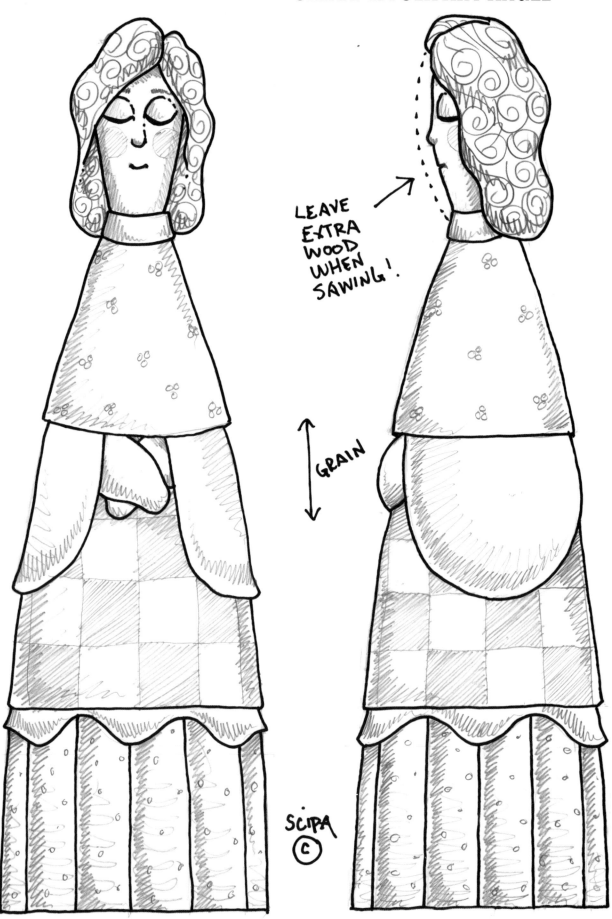

LEAVE
EXTRA
WOOD
WHEN
SAWING!

GRAIN

SCIPA
©

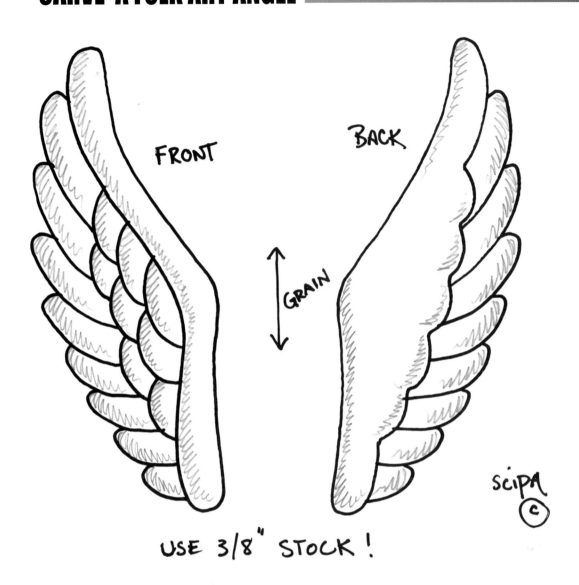

FRONT

BACK

GRAIN

SCiPA ©

USE 3/8" STOCK !

IDEAS...

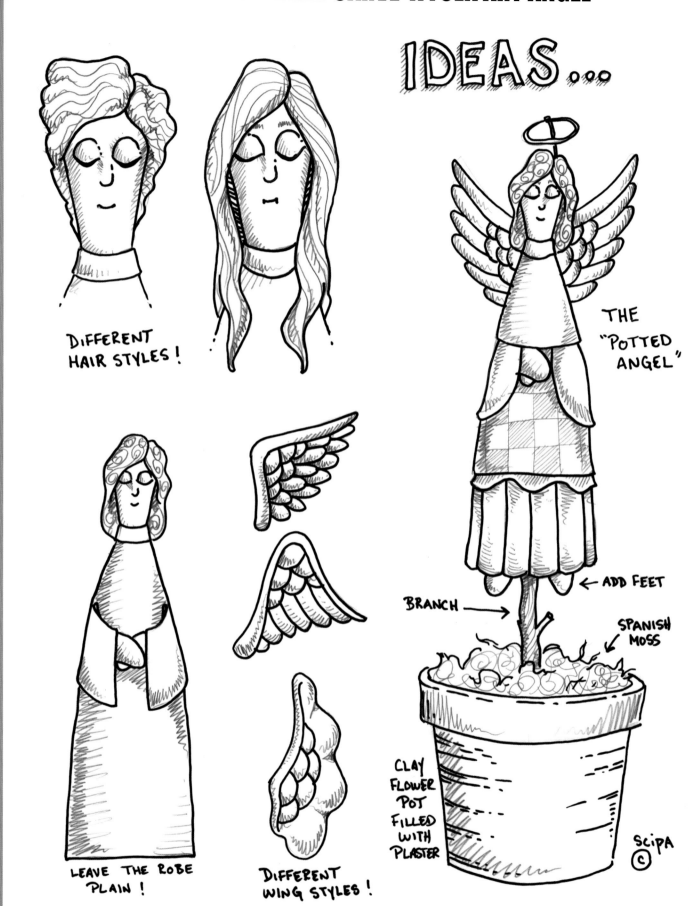

DIFFERENT HAIR STYLES!

LEAVE THE ROBE PLAIN!

DIFFERENT WING STYLES!

THE "POTTED ANGEL"

← ADD FEET

BRANCH →

SPANISH MOSS

CLAY FLOWER POT FILLED WITH PLASTER

SCIPA ©

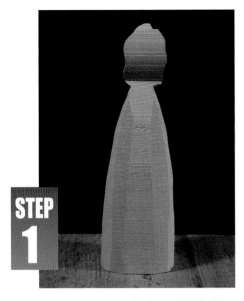

STEP 1

The front view of the bandsawed blank. The body has a very simple shape, making it easy to saw off the hard corners. Leave the head intact for now; it's too easy to take off too much.

STEP 2

The side view. When tracing the pattern, be sure to leave a little extra on the facial profile.

STEP 3

Using a larger rough-out knife, knock off the corners and round out the body up to the neck. Be sure not to thin out the neck too much at this point.

STEP 4

The body is smoothed out and all saw marks are "erased." The view from the underside should be more or less like a circle. Leave the head untouched for now.

STEP 5

Referring to the pattern, draw a line for the shawl all the way around the body.

STEP 6

Using the knife, make a stop cut along the line.

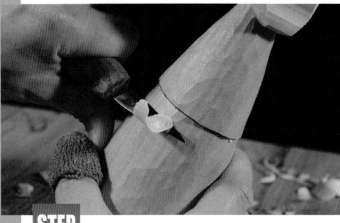

STEP 7 Taper the body up to the stop cut, working all the way around. Make the shawl look about 1/8-inch thick.

STEP 8 Draw in lines for the second layer of the shawl, referring to the pattern as needed.

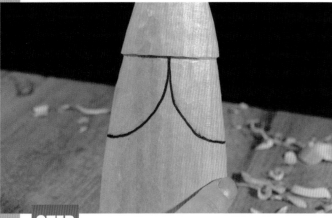

STEP 9 Draw in the back of the second shawl.

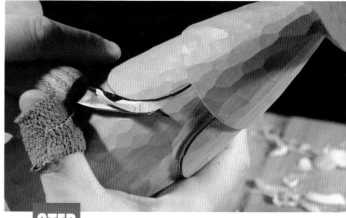

STEP 10 Make stop cuts along these lines and again taper the body up. Leave some wood in front where the hands will go.

STEP 11 With the knife, scallop the second shawl a little to give it some form. Work it all the way around.

STEP 12 Draw in the overlapped hands, referring to the pattern as a guide.

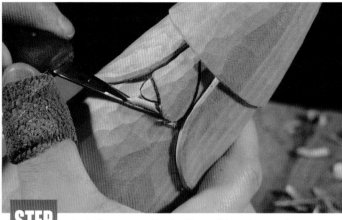

STEP 13

Switch to a smaller knife at this point. Make stop cuts along the lines of the hands and remove wood from below, leaving the hands about one quarter of an inch thick. Be sure to taper up the body and smooth out the area.

STEP 14

Separate the hands and round them out, giving them shape.

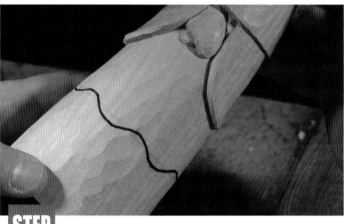

STEP 15

The hands are complete. Next, draw in the wavy line as shown around the body. Refer to the pattern for the position. This will be the ruffle on the top layer of the angel's dress.

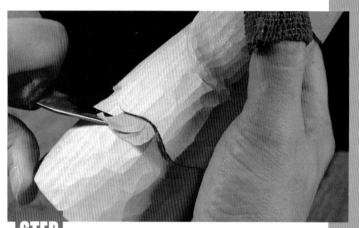

STEP 16

Still using the knife, make a stop cut and remove wood from below the stop, tapering up from the bottom. Work it all the way around.

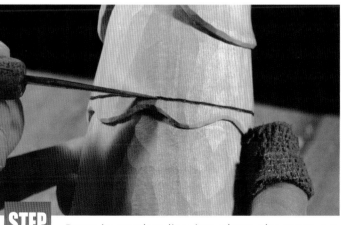

STEP 17

Draw in another line just above the wavy cut. Make a stop cut along this line.

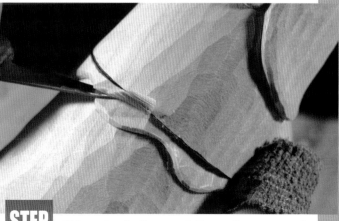

STEP 18

Using the knife, carefully scallop out each "ruffle" as shown. Lightly scoop out wood in each section, using the stop cut you just created. This makes it look like she has a ruffled trim emerging from under her upper skirt.

STEP 19
Draw in vertical lines from the ruffle down to the bottom. Make them about three quarters of an inch apart, or whatever distance works out even for you.

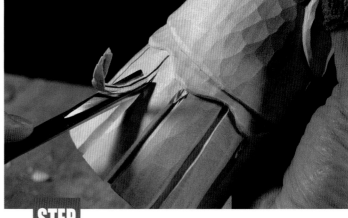

STEP 20
Using a #12 v-tool, cut trenches in the skirt. Use the lines as center marks, being careful not to mar the ruffle. Try to keep the depth even all the way around.

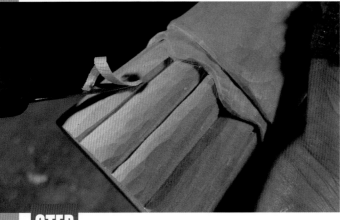

STEP 21
Using the knife, round off the edge of each v-cut and clean up under the ruffles. This is to create a pleated skirt effect with "puffy" segments.

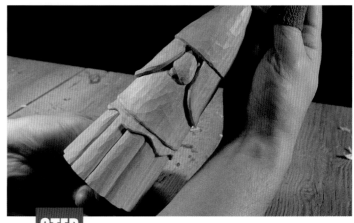

STEP 22
Progress so far. The body is complete! Be sure to slightly bevel any hard edges you may have created.

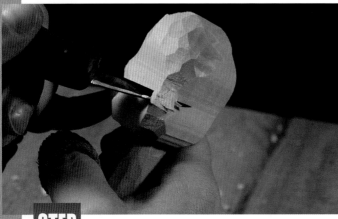

STEP 23
Now for the angel's head. Using the knife, round off the corners in back. Leave the front alone for now.

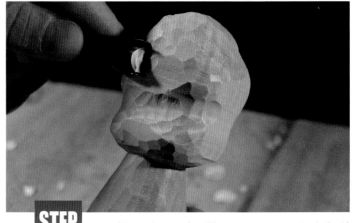

STEP 24
At this point, I also like to use a 1/2-inch half round gouge to help create and maintain the peaks and valleys in her hair.

STEP 25
The back of the head is shaped and ready for detail.

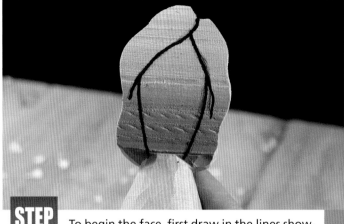

STEP 26
To begin the face, first draw in the lines showing the shape of the head and the hairlines over the forehead, as shown.

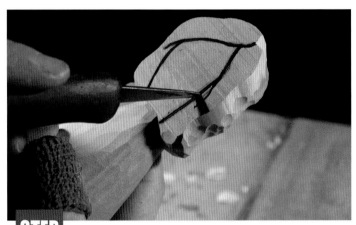

STEP 27
Using the knife, make deep plunge cuts straight in. Don't angle the knifepoint toward the face. Try to get it as deep as you can on the first pass in order to keep the cut clean.

STEP 28
Begin to pare away small amounts of wood on both sides of the cuts to separate the face from the hair. Avoid taking too much from the very front of the face at this point.

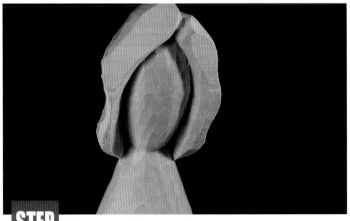

STEP 29
Progress so far. I have gone deep into the sides of the face with the knife, maintaining the neck/collar line as I go. The part in her hair is forming. I have also shaped the face like an egg. This face design—with a button nose and closed, reverent eyes—is stylized and very simple.

STEP 30
Now that the face is somewhat defined, shape the front locks of hair with the knife. Further define the part. Cut back on the lower portion of the hair a little; this will help reveal the profile from the side.

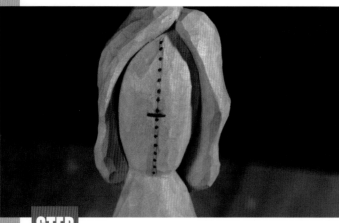

STEP 31
The hair is defined better and closer to its final shape. Find the center of the face and make a mark halfway down, as shown.

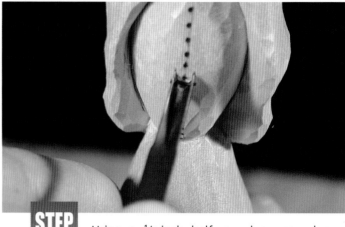

STEP 32
Using a 1/8-inch half round gouge, plunge straight into the face. Make sure the bottom of the gouge is placed right above the half way mark.

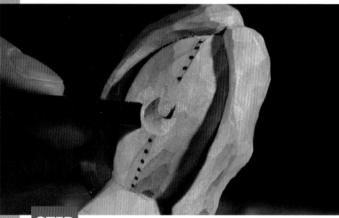

STEP 33
Using a 1/4-inch shallow gouge, hollow out a pocket below the plunge cut. Again, be careful not to chip out the nose.

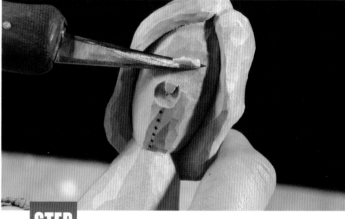

STEP 34
Using the knife, slightly scallop out wood above the nose to create a bridge slope. Follow through to the hairline.

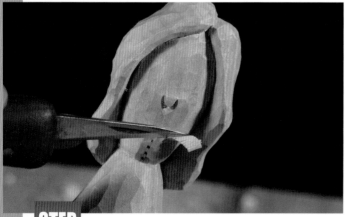

STEP 35
Now remove wood from the sides and bottom, to "erase" the hollow under the nose. This action brings out the button nose, and makes it the most prominent point on the face.

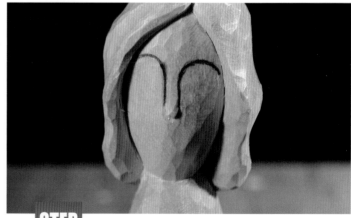

STEP 36
Draw in the hollows of the eyes, as shown.

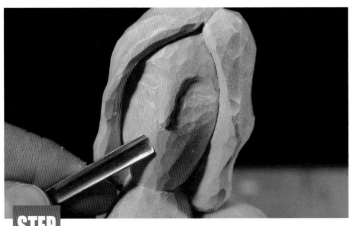

STEP 37

Using the ¼-inch shallow gouge, hollow out these eye areas. This helps to form the nose and the brow.

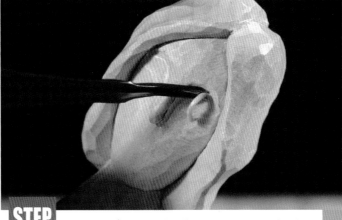

STEP 38

Using a ¹⁄₁₆-inch half round gouge, further define the nose and brow, as shown. Clean up the nose, soften the brow, and round the bridge. Her eyes will be closed, so draw in the eyelids.

STEP 39

Use small stop cuts to remove a slice of wood below the eyelids, as shown.

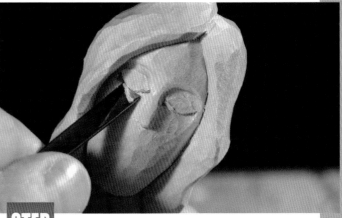

STEP 40

Using the ¼-inch shallow gouge, taper the cheeks a little up to the eyelids. This completes the eyes and nose.

STEP 41

Thin down the lower half of the face with the knife and draw in the upturned mouth. Cut the mouth like the eyes. To open up the mouth, plunge the tip of the knife into each corner of the mouth, with the spine of the knife facing outwards. This will compress the wood fibers and open up the mouth.

STEP 42

The face is completed—simple yet effective. Draw in the collar.

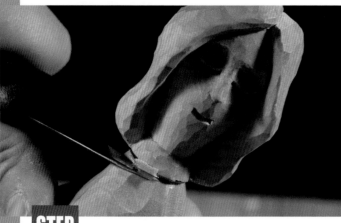

STEP 43

Use the knife to define the collar, using stop and taper cuts.

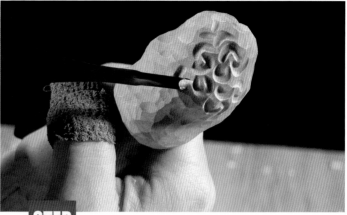

STEP 44

Using the ¼-inch half round gouge, create texture in the hair. I like to apply tight circles, which gives the hair a curly effect.

STEP 45

The hair is complete.

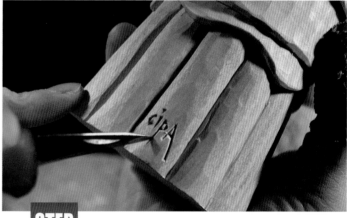

STEP 46

Sign your carving! Luckily, I was blessed with only four letters in my name.

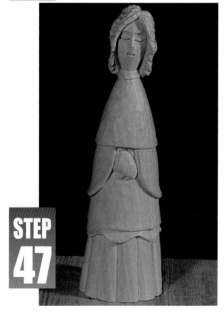

STEP 47

The angel's body is complete.

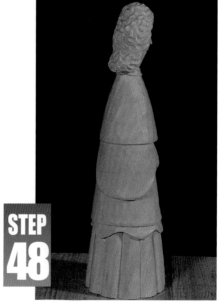

STEP 48

A side view. Now for the wings. Remember, she is an angel!

STEP 1
These are the sawed blanks of the angel's wings. The patterns show one wing, front and back. For the second wing, simply invert the pattern.

STEP 2
Referring to your pattern, draw in the "spine" of the wing. Begin with the front view.

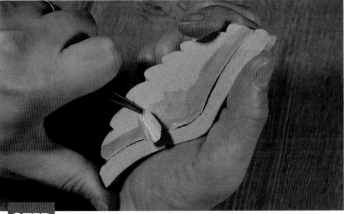

STEP 3
Using the knife, make a stop cut and remove wood from the larger area. Also round off the "spine."

STEP 4
Draw in the first inner feather.

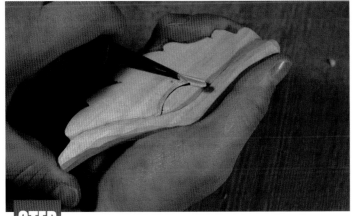

STEP 5
Make a stop cut and remove wood around it.

STEP 6
Draw in the next layer, two feathers this time, like so.

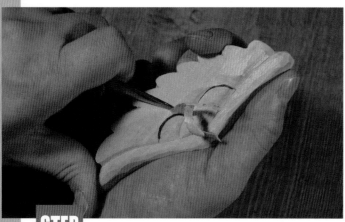

STEP 7

Once again, stop cut and remove more wood. Do you see a pattern developing? Try to keep the feathers thin, so that you don't run out of wood. Remember, the wing is only 3/8 inch thick, and you have to carve the other side yet.

STEP 8

The third layer.

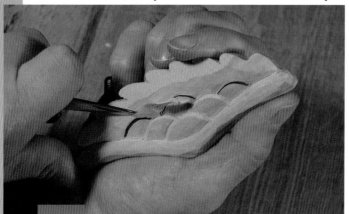

STEP 9

You know the drill.

STEP 10

The last layer of inner feathers. Be sure to bevel the edges of them with the knife as you go.

STEP 11

Once the inner feathers are complete, draw in the long feathers as shown.

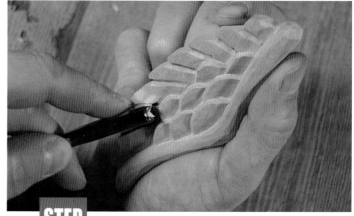

STEP 12

Using the #12 v-tool, separate each feather along the lines. Avoid going too deep. You don't want to go through the other side.

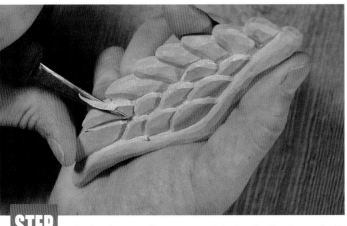

STEP 13
Go back over the v-cuts with the knife. Round off the edges and clean up each feather.

STEP 14
The front side is complete.

STEP 15
On to the back side. Not having as much detail, the outer portion of the wing is all one piece. Draw it in, as shown.

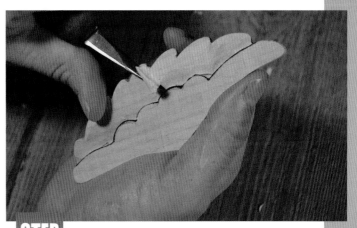

STEP 16
Make a stop cut and remove wood with the knife from the long feathered portion. Keep it shallow.

STEP 17
Remove the saw marks from the outer portion and round off the hard edge on the spine.

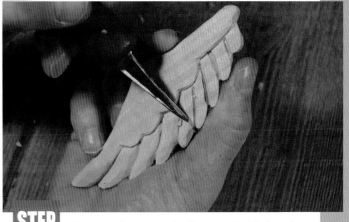

STEP 18
Repeat the steps in Photos 10–12 for the long feathers. The wood is getting thinner, so be careful.

CARVE A FOLK ART ANGEL

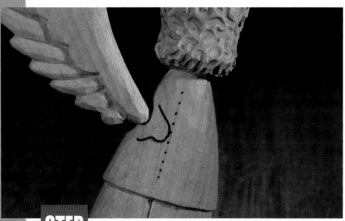

STEP 19
On the angel's back, find and mark the center. Take one wing (remember, small feathers towards the front), place it where you want it to be, and trace the tip onto the surface.

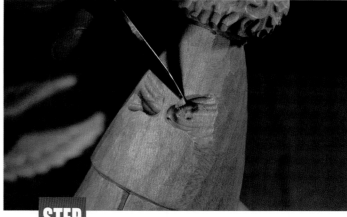

STEP 20
Using a gouge of your choice, scoop out a pocket for the wing tip. Take small amounts to get a perfect fit. Do the other side, making sure it is even with the first wing.

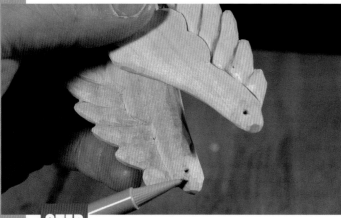

STEP 21
Before attaching the wings, make sure you pre-drill very small holes, as shown. If you skip this step, you will almost certainly split the wood on the tip while inserting the nail.

STEP 22
Apply a small amount of glue into one pocket.

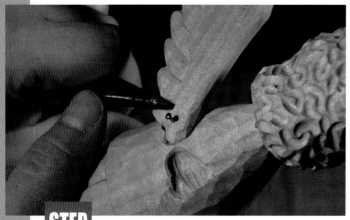

STEP 23
Place the wing in its pocket and push in the nail, using the pliers. The wood is soft enough to do this; you shouldn't need a hammer. Push the nail in flush with the surface. Attach the other wing.

STEP 24
Both wings attached. Wipe off any excess glue immediately with a damp cloth. Let dry overnight before painting.

STEP 1

Before painting, lightly clean your carving with mild dishwashing soap and a toothbrush to remove oils from your hands. Once it has dried, pencil in light guidelines for the checkerboard pattern.

STEP 2

Using a large flat brush, paint her shawl an olive green.

STEP 3

For the collar, sleeves and ruffled trim, use titanium white. I use the large brush for the sleeves and a smaller round brush for the collar and trim. Apply the white a little thicker than the other colors.

STEP 4

For the bottom skirt, apply antique white with the large brush.

STEP 5

Use sage green for half of the checkerboard pattern on the upper skirt. Apply the color with the small round brush.

STEP 6

For the other half of the checkerboard pattern, use mint green.

PAINT A FOLK ART ANGEL

STEP 7

Using the small round brush, paint the face and hands with flesh tone.

STEP 8

Mixing a bit of bright red with the flesh tone, add rosy cheeks by blending the mixed color into the already wet surface. Add a touch of the mixture to the eyelids and lips as well.

STEP 9

This angel is going to be a redhead, so I begin with cinnamon. Paint the main area with the larger brush, but use the small round brush to get in around the face.

STEP 10

Using the small brush, highlight the hair with tangerine orange.

STEP 11

Next, I paint the wings gold using the large brush. You can paint them white if you like; I prefer gold with this color scheme. If you get the right shade, it will look similar to gold leafing after it is antiqued.

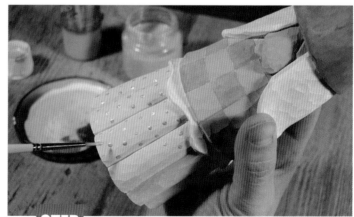

STEP 12

While you have the gold paint out, apply a dot pattern on the bottom skirt. Use a small detail brush for this.

STEP 13

For interest, apply a dot pattern to the shawl as well. Here I am using the mint green.

STEP 14

Finally, a few details to the face. Using the cinnamon and a very fine detail brush, paint in the eyebrows. Also, add eyelashes by following the curve of the eyelid. When the painting is complete, let the angel dry for one hour.

STEP 15

Seal the carving with satin polyurethane. Using a stain brush, apply the sealer as thin as possible, scrubbing into the nooks. This will seal the carving for the antique process.

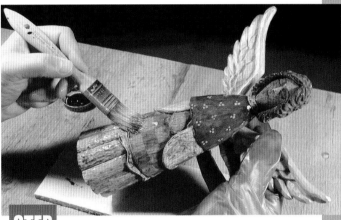

STEP 16

Apply the antique gel wood stain, slathering it on so it gets into the crevices.

STEP 17

Immediately wipe away the excess with a clean cotton cloth (an old tee shirt works great!). Let the carving dry overnight before handling it.

STEP 18

Construct a halo from craft wire. Drill a small hole in the back of her head near the top and insert the halo stem with a little instant crazy glue. Let it dry for a few minutes and bend the halo where you like it. Your angel is complete!

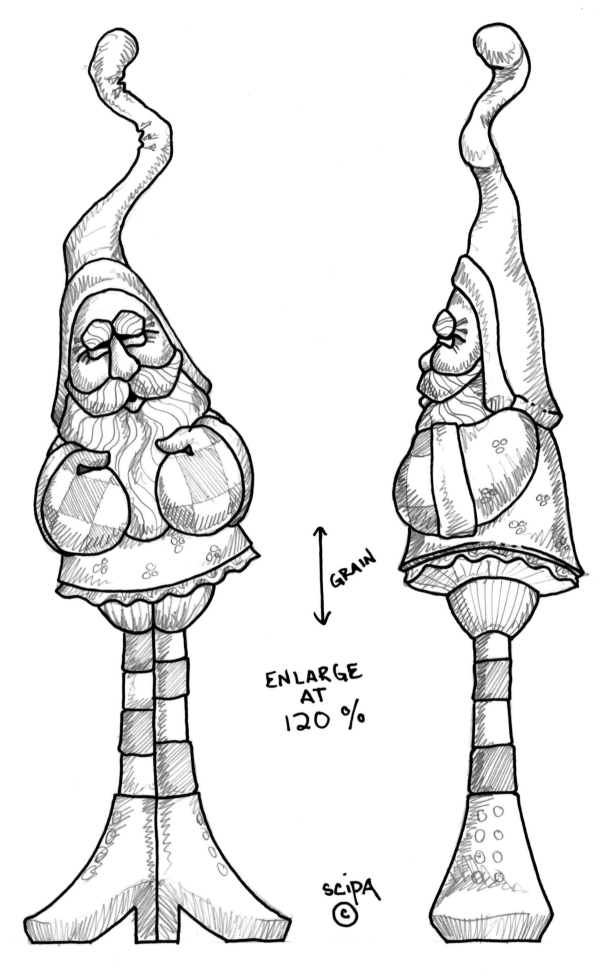

GRAIN

ENLARGE
AT
120 %

SCIPA©

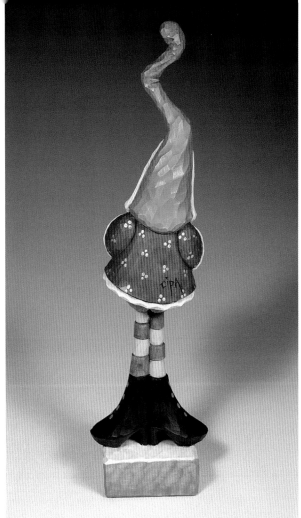

Long Legs

I enjoy carving this one a lot.
He's a very happy guy and whimsical to boot.
The pattern is reduced to fit on the page.
You could easily carve him the size shown, but I prefer
to make him about 20 percent larger than that.
The carving shown here was created from
a 3½" x 2½" x 12" block. Bandsawing this pattern
is a little tricky around the legs; be sure to leave stock
for the puffy "pantaloons" emerging from under his coat.
For fun, try extending the legs to suit your taste.
One thing you will notice is that I have mounted him
on a small block of wood. This is necessary
for his stability; the feet aren't wide enough
to allow him to stand on his own.

Pattern on page 44.

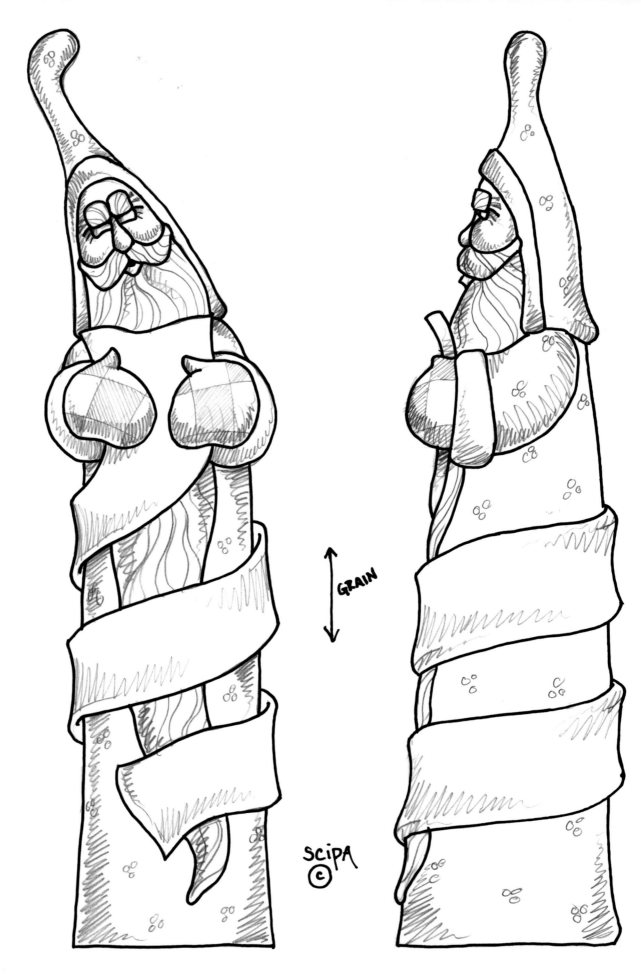

GRAIN

SCIPA ©

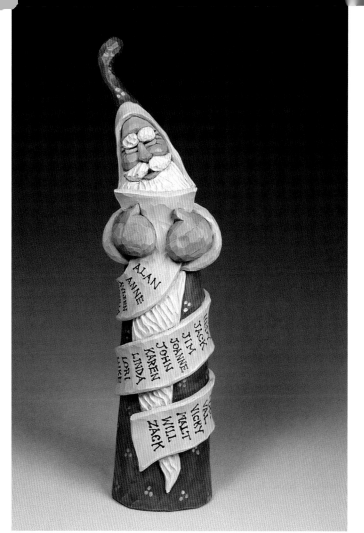

Santa's List

This guy makes a great gift for friends and family. By painting in the respective names on the list, you can personalize your carving. The block measures $2^1/_2$" x $2^1/_2$"x 10". The great thing about this carving is that you can extend the body for drama, while providing much more room for names. I carved a Santa similar to this one for a good customer of mine and left the list extra long by her request. Having a large family, she asks me to add names from time to time, whenever someone gets married or has a new arrival! How big is your family?

Pattern on page 46.

BACK GRAIN

GRAIN FRONT

DRILL
¼" HOLES
IN BACK
AND
INSERT WINGS

DRILL
HOLE
FOR
WIRE LOOP

GRAIN

SCIPA
E

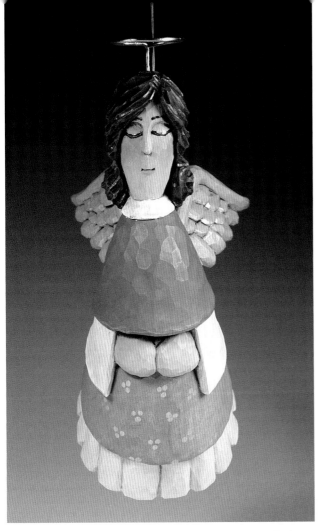

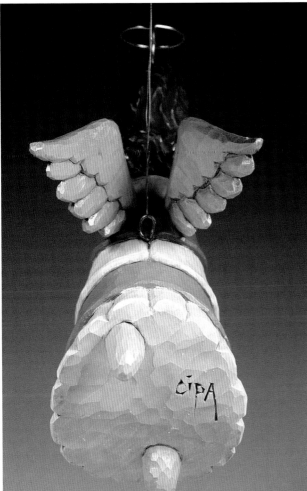

Flying Angel

This angel should be displayed
by hanging her from a wire or string,
as if she were flying about.
The block measures $3^3/_4$" x $3^3/_4$" x $8^1/_2$".
The wings cut are from $^3/_8$-inch-thick stock.
When carving the wings, round off the ends
and insert them into $^1/_4$-inch holes drilled
into her back. Glue the wings in place.
Also add a small hanger made
from some stiff 12-gauge copper wire.
Be sure to use some two-part epoxy glue
for this, because the wire needs
to support the weight of the carving.

Pattern on page 48.

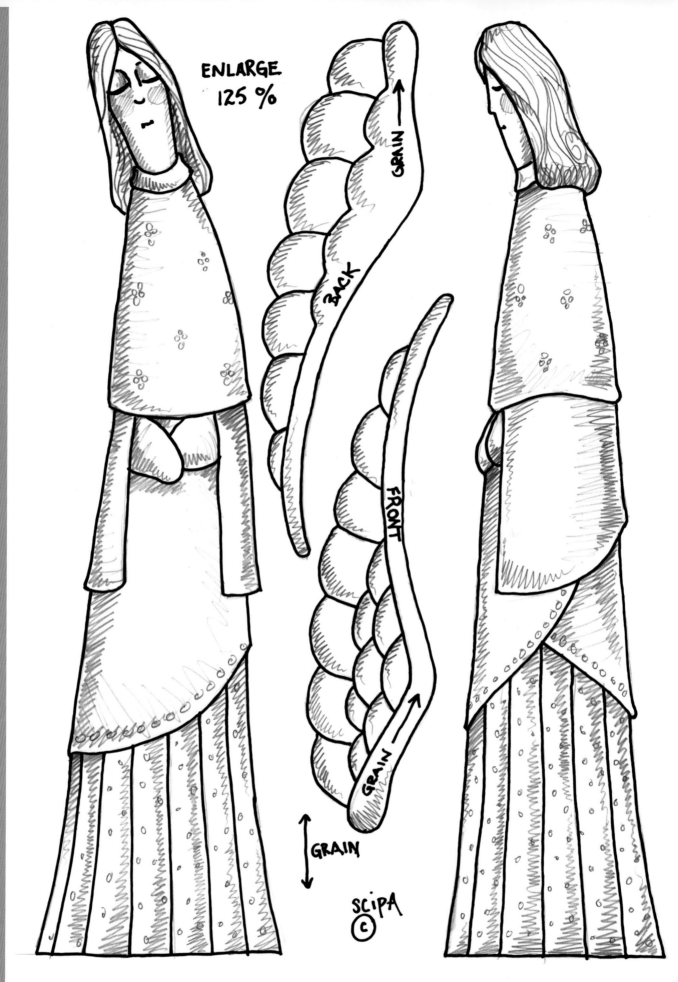

ENLARGE
125 %

GRAIN

BACK

FRONT

GRAIN

GRAIN

SCIPA
©

Tall Angel

This angel is a favorite.
Measuring 14 inches tall (16 inches with the wings),
the pattern has been reduced to fit the page.
Feel free to carve the pattern as shown,
but it is much more impressive to increase
the size by about 25 percent.
What's even better is to lengthen her body
for a more dramatic effect.
Add the length from below the sleeves.
If you do this, be sure to maintain
the slight curving of the overall figure.
This helps to retain expression of the piece.
The block measures 4" x 3½" x 14".
The wings are cut from ³⁄₈-inch-thick stock.

Pattern on page 50.

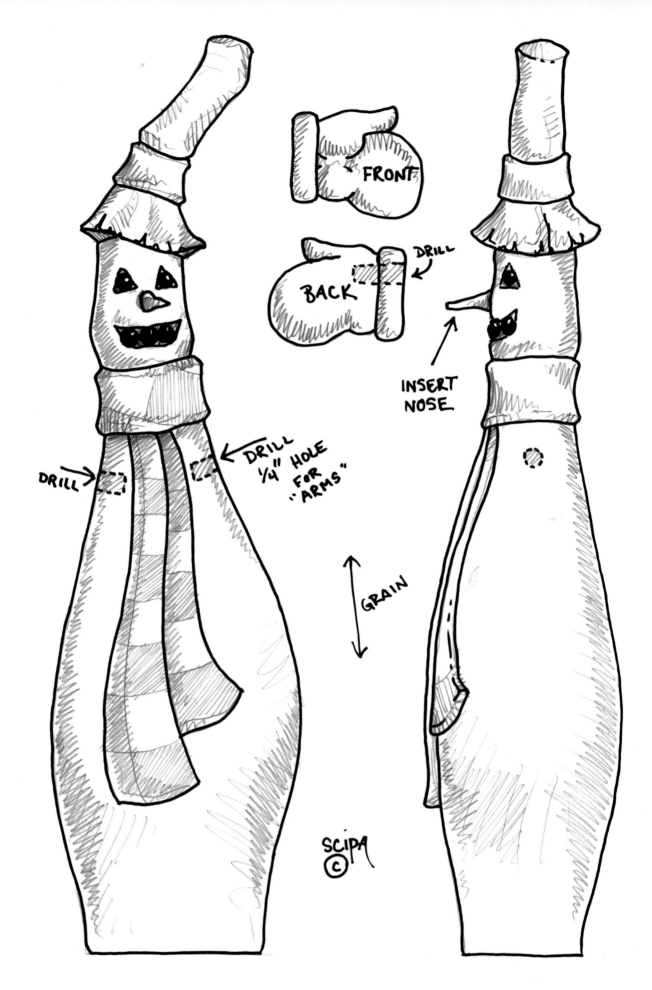

FRONT

BACK

DRILL

INSERT
NOSE

DRILL

DRILL
1/4" HOLE
FOR
"ARMS"

GRAIN

SCIPA ©

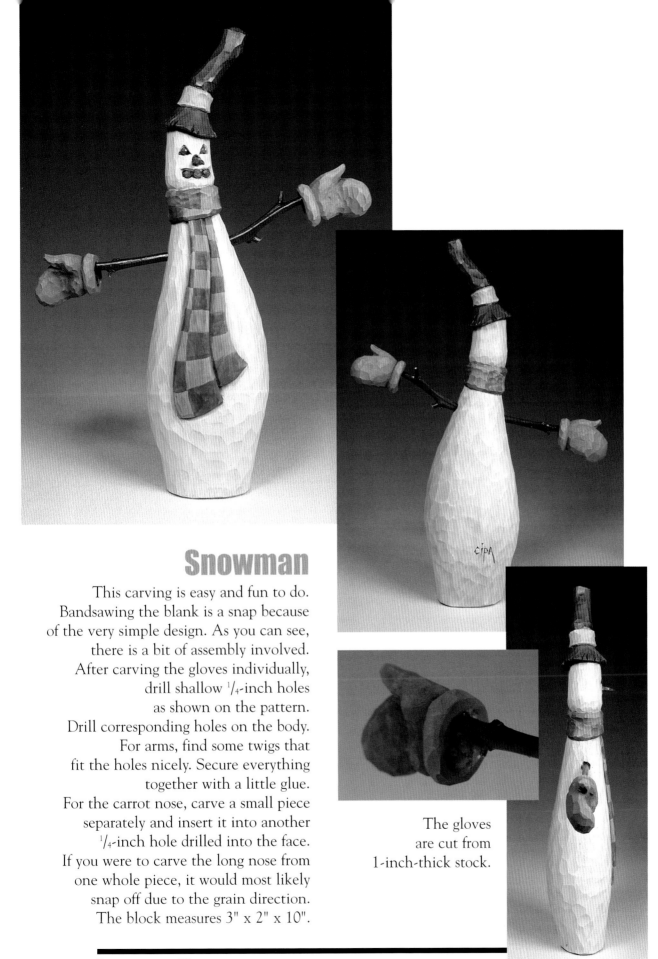

Snowman

This carving is easy and fun to do.
Bandsawing the blank is a snap because
of the very simple design. As you can see,
there is a bit of assembly involved.
After carving the gloves individually,
drill shallow ¼-inch holes
as shown on the pattern.
Drill corresponding holes on the body.
For arms, find some twigs that
fit the holes nicely. Secure everything
together with a little glue.
For the carrot nose, carve a small piece
separately and insert it into another
¼-inch hole drilled into the face.
If you were to carve the long nose from
one whole piece, it would most likely
snap off due to the grain direction.
The block measures 3" x 2" x 10".

The gloves
are cut from
1-inch-thick stock.

Pattern on page 52.

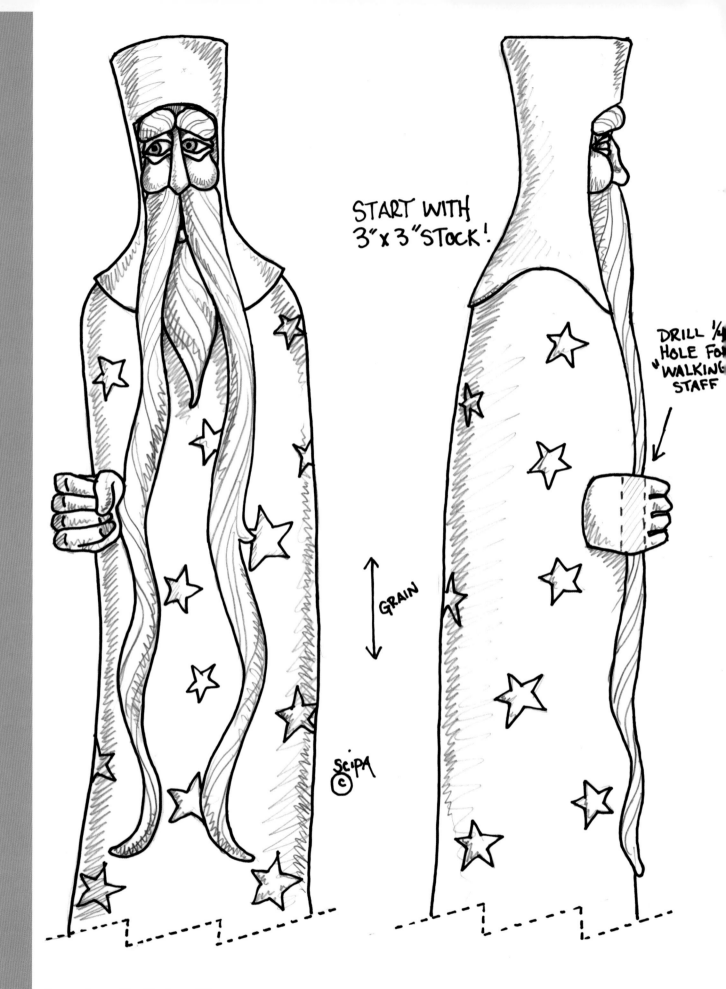

START WITH
3" x 3" STOCK!

DRILL ¼"
HOLE FOR
WALKING
STAFF

GRAIN

SCIPA ©

Wizard

You can probably tell by now that I like to create a lot of long, thin designs. This guy is no exception. I have only provided the upper half of the pattern for this project. He is much too tall (18 inches high) to reduce, and there is hardly any detail below his mustache. Besides, I encourage you to make his body as long as you like—the longer the better! That was the point of the whole design.

Just remember to avoid making the body straight and stiff. Be sure that he leans a little this way and that. Why only one hand showing? It is a stylized piece, and I took artistic license by eliminating the other hand; I felt that the second hand would interrupt the "flow." The hand that is showing is carved from the same block, not inserted. Keep that in mind when sawing out the blank. Drill a $\frac{1}{4}$-inch hole through the hand to insert his walking staff, making sure the staff is as long as it takes to reach the bottom of the carving. Carve the stick as you please or find an unusual twisted branch instead. The block measures 3" x 3" x as long as you want. Carve several wizards of varying heights and display them together, as if they were conferring over very "wizardly" matters!

Pattern on page 54.

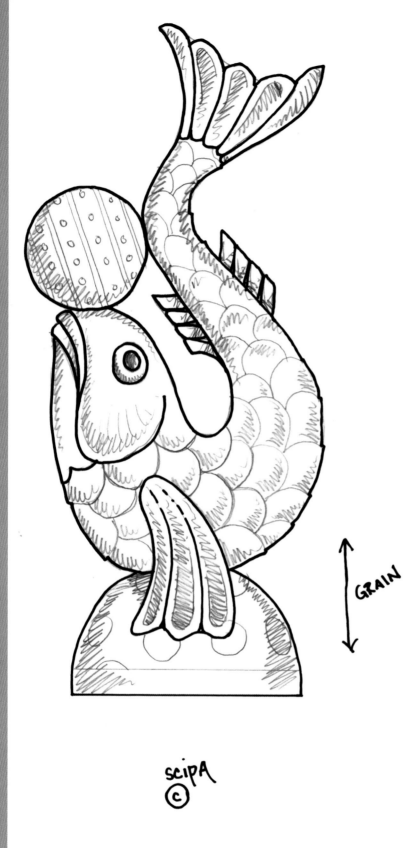

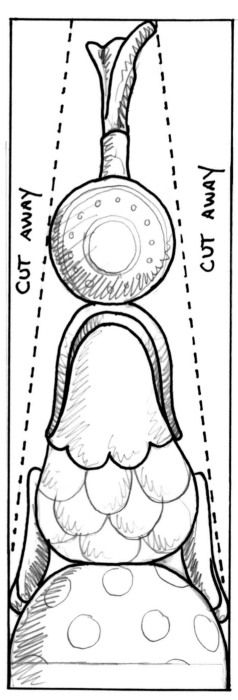

USE 2½"
THICK
STOCK!

GRAIN

CUT AWAY

CUT AWAY

SCIPA
©

Circus Fish

Silly, isn't it? I could have carved a seal or an elephant or even a bear. But people have seen those things. Who ever heard of a circus fish? Actually, the idea was inspired by some ancient sculpture I had seen in a book somewhere. The ball was really a world globe and the fish represented the Cosmos, supporting the Earth in Space. I decidedly made it more light-hearted. More importantly, this design is an excellent lesson in form. Take care when sawing out the blank. The void in the middle can be handled two ways: 1) When sawing, carefully enter the area between the ball and the tail, keeping the kerf to a minimum; or 2) simply leave it whole and remove the wood by knife as you carve. Either way, this carving is great practice. You can either carve the scales individually, as I have done, or you can leave the surface smooth and paint them on. The block measures 3 ½" x 2 ½" x 7 ½". This project would also be great on a much larger scale with added detail.

Pattern on page 56.

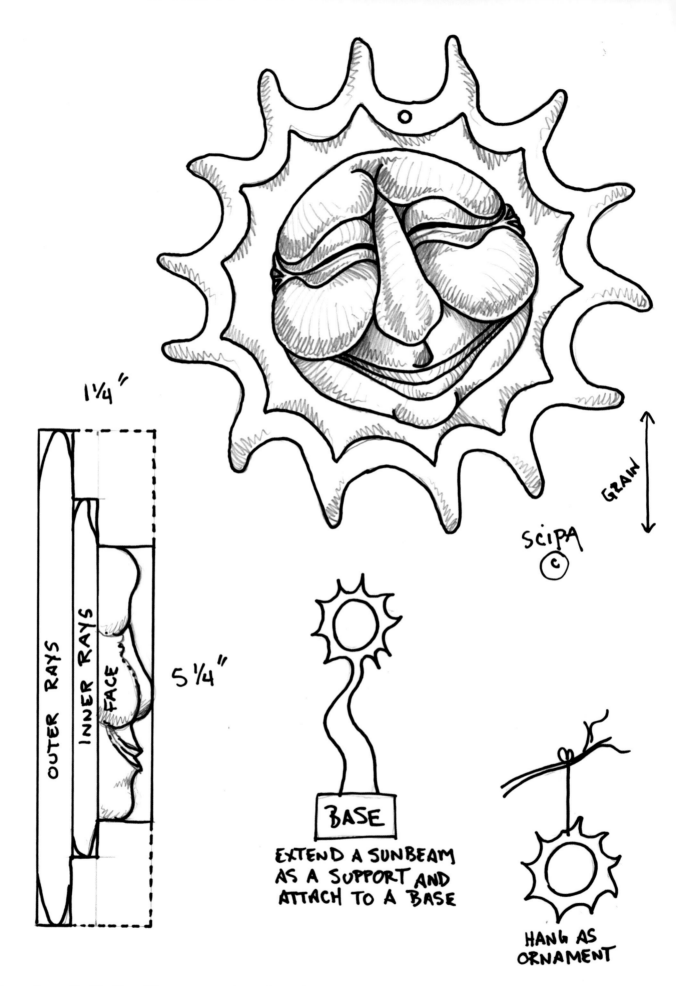

1¼"

5¼"

OUTER RAYS

INNER RAYS

FACE

GRAIN

SCIPA ©

BASE

EXTEND A SUNBEAM
AS A SUPPORT AND
ATTACH TO A BASE

HANG AS
ORNAMENT

Fat Old Sun

This guy will brighten up a gloomy day!
This carving is more or less a relief carving,
with detail only on one side.
As the suggestions on the pattern will show,
he can either be displayed as an ornament
or as a freestanding piece. To make an
ornament, attach a wire loop. To make a
freestanding piece, extend the bottom
sunbeam and attach it to a base block.
Use woodscrews inserted from underneath.
The block measures $5\frac{1}{2}$" x $5\frac{1}{2}$" x $1\frac{1}{4}$".

Pattern on page 58.

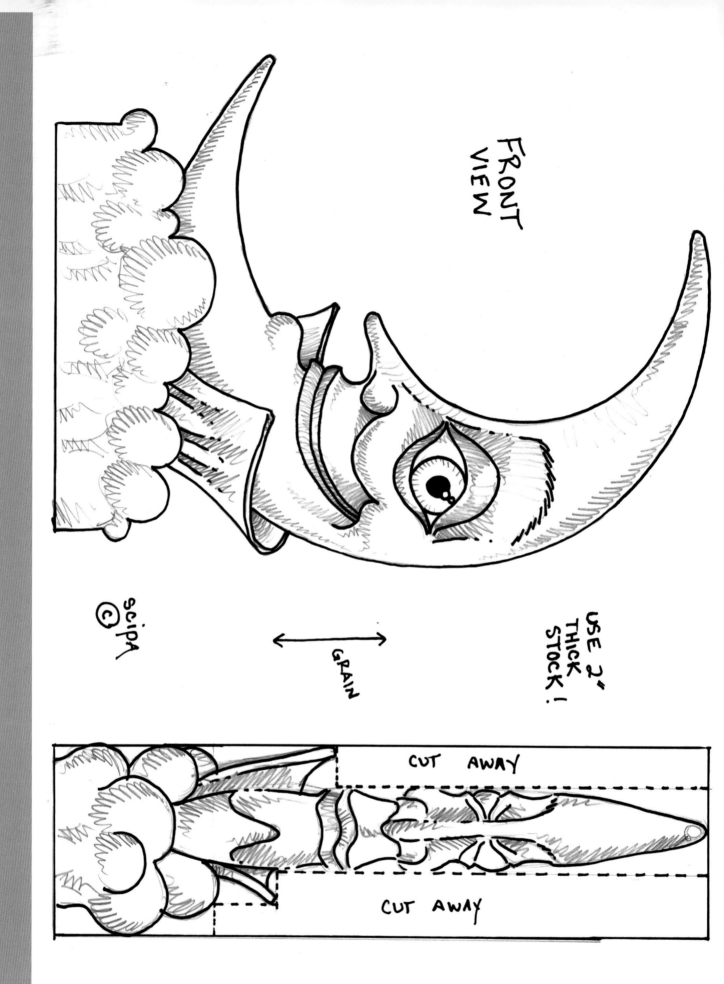

FRONT VIEW

© scipa

GRAIN

USE 2"
THICK
STOCK!

CUT AWAY

CUT AWAY

Moon Man

This carving requires a little more skill to complete. Although it is practically a relief carving, both sides are carved and they are different from each other. The trick is to blend the details together on the edges. You will need to use some gouges, as well as a knife, to complete this project.

Take care when hollowing out the areas between his face and collar. The block measures 7" x 6 ½" x 2". If you're feeling ambitious, this carving would look great as a much larger piece. Say, about, 12 inches or 13 inches high?

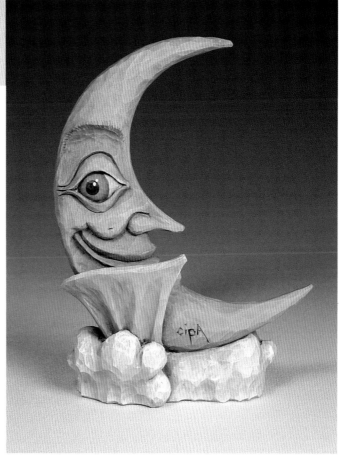

Patterns on pages 60 and 62.

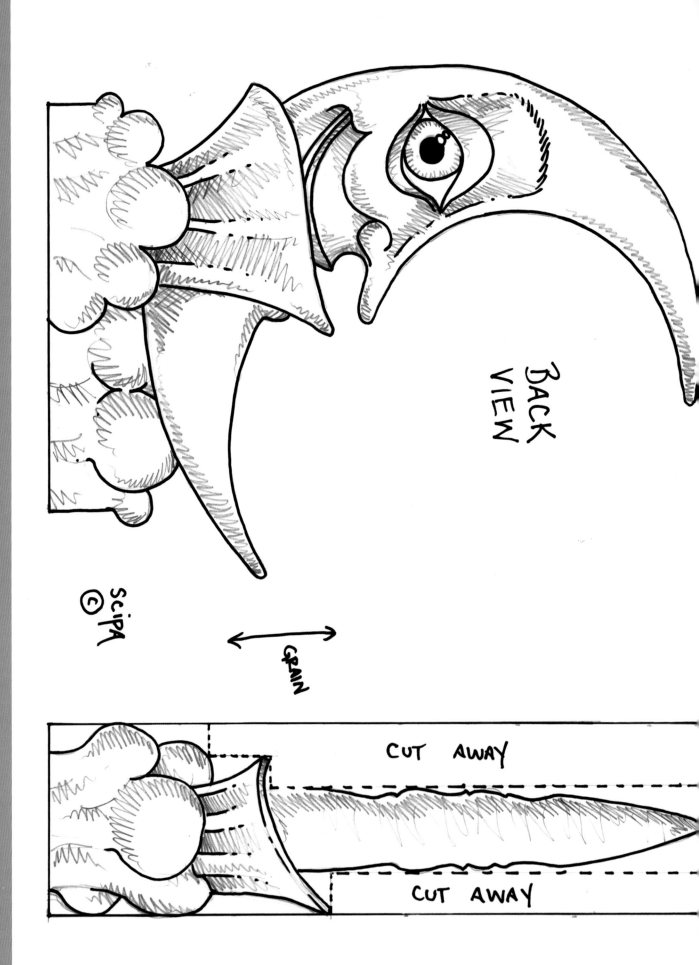

BACK
VIEW

©
ScIPA

GRAIN

CUT AWAY

CUT AWAY

Pattern on pages 64 and 65.

Firewood Santa

Santa gets cold too! He is shown here gathering wood for the fireplace. You will need to drill a $^1/_4$" hole in his glove to insert a walking staff. The staff can be carved from stock, or you could simply find a stick that fits the hole. Secure the staff with a drop of glue. You will also need to hollow out the sack (a spoon gouge helps) in order to insert small sticks as the "firewood." I just squeeze out a small pool of glue in the bottom and place each stick in until the sack is filled up. You could also hollow the sack out deeper and use the carving to hold matches on your fireplace mantel. The block measures $4^1/_2$" x 2" x 10". Notice the attached base for stability.

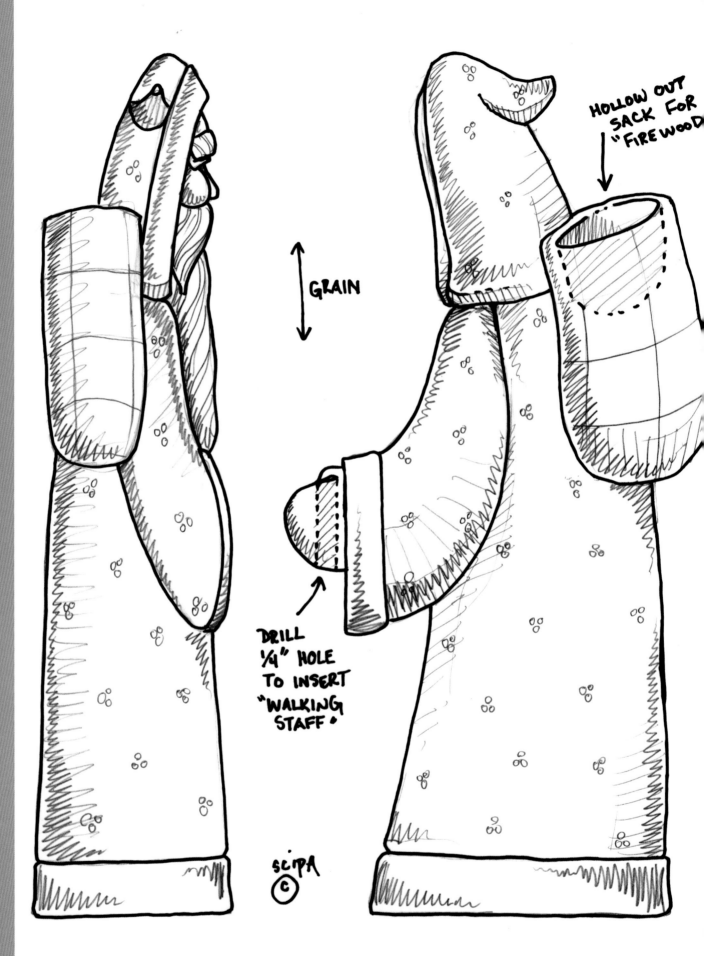

GRAIN

HOLLOW OUT
SACK FOR
"FIREWOOD"

DRILL
1/4" HOLE
TO INSERT
"WALKING
STAFF"

SCIPA
©

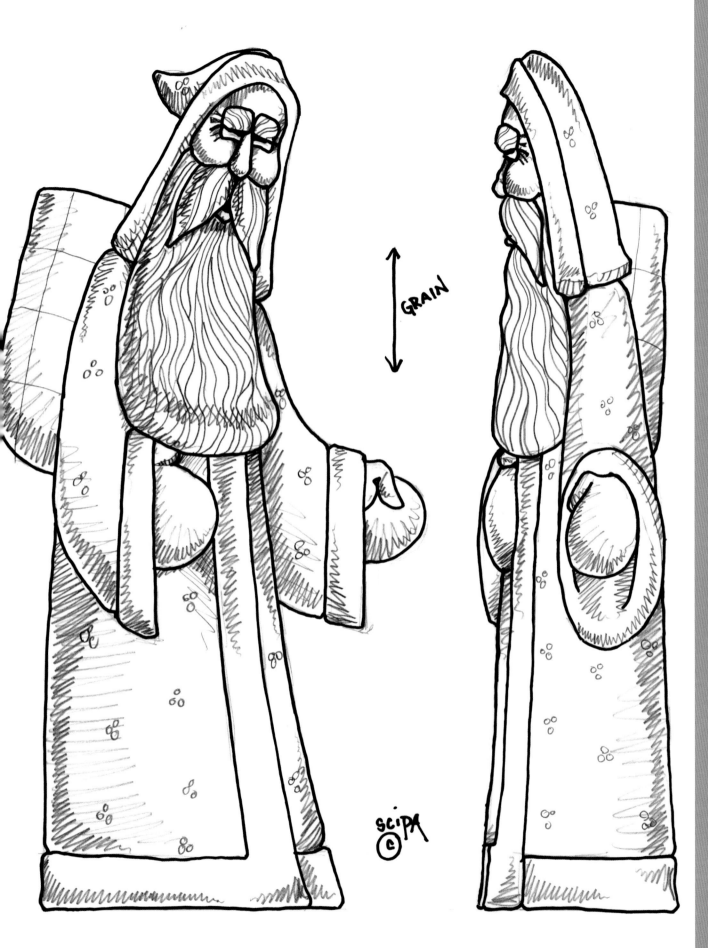

GRAIN

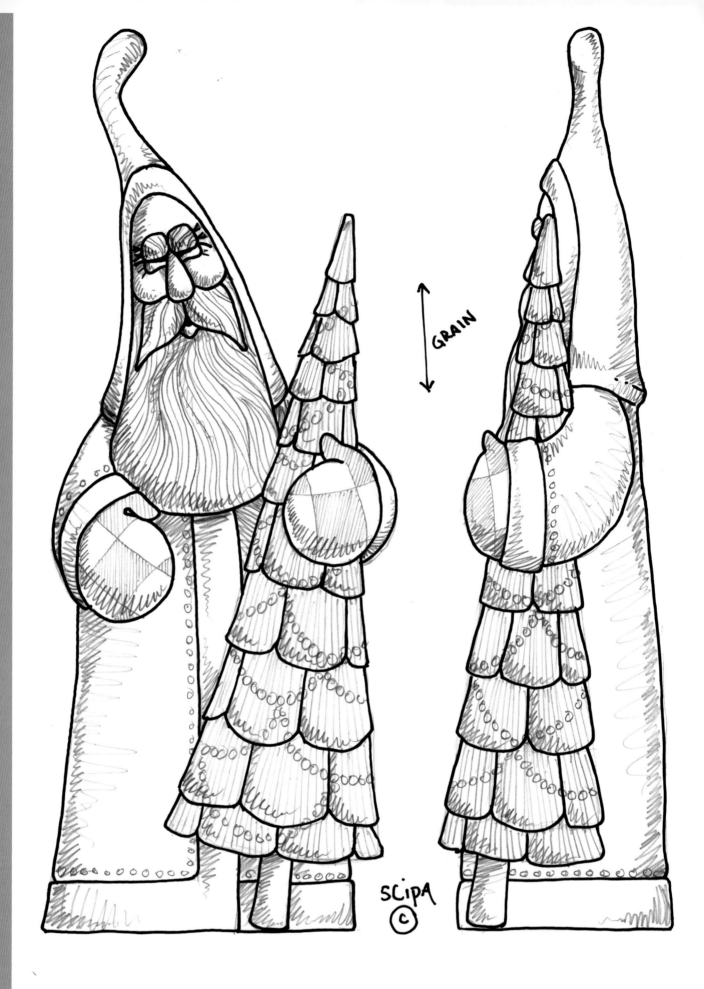

GRAIN

SCiPA ©

Tree Santa

Santa brings home the Christmas tree!
This pattern is easy to band saw;
the stock is only 2$\frac{1}{2}$ inches thick.
Carving him is a bit of a challenge.
Make sure to maintain the correct
proportion of the arm wrapping
around the tree.
It's easy to take off too much here.
The block measures 4" x 2$\frac{1}{2}$" x 10".
Although he will stand fine
on his own, I have added a base
to complete the piece.

Pattern on pages 66 and 68.

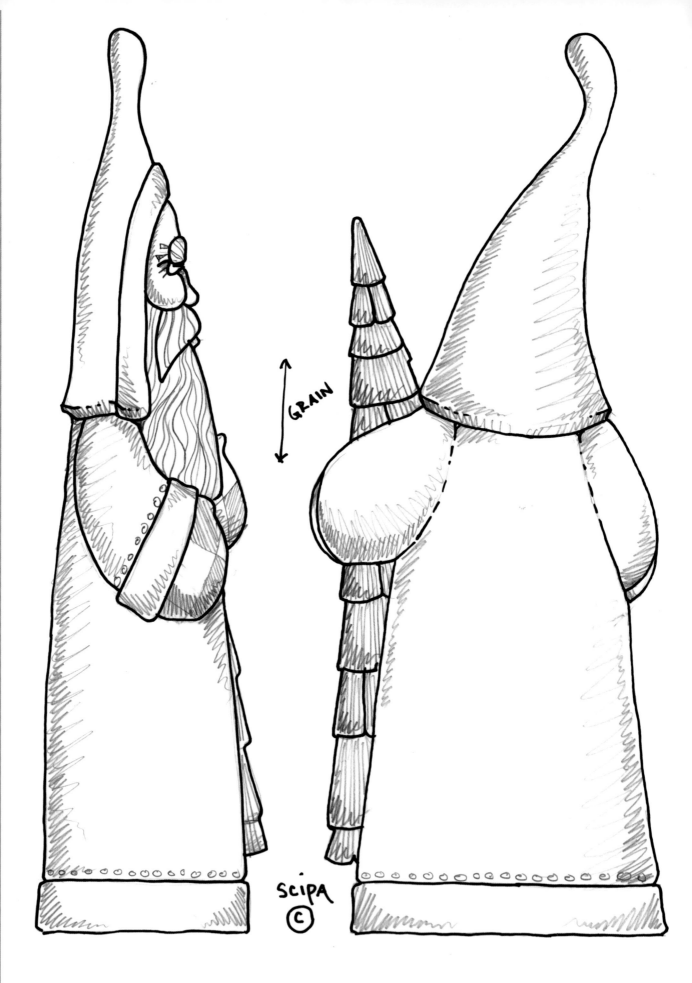

GRAIN

SCIPA ©

Starry Angel

This Angel's design is similar to the Firewood Santa, except that
she is holding a star in her hand. Refer back to the step-by step angel
when attaching the wings and halo. Carve the star out of ¼-inch-thick stock,
and drill a very small hole in one point. Hollow out a small niche in her hand
where the star will fit. Attach the star with a small wire nail and a bit of glue.
The block measures 4" x 3½" x 9", The wings are cut from ⅜" stock.

Pattern on pages 70 and 71.

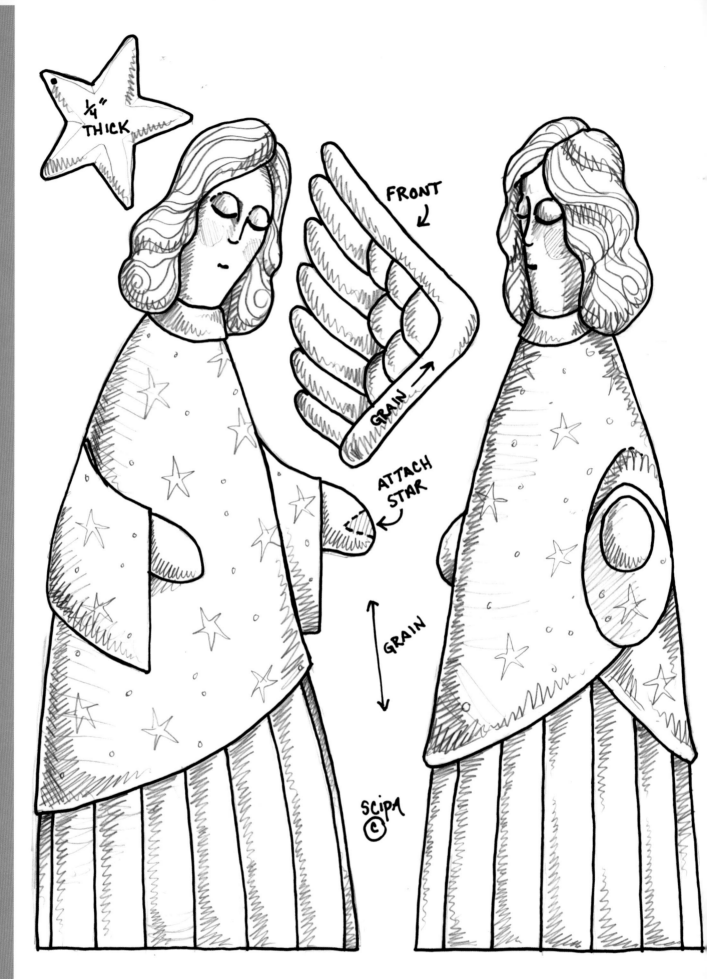

¼" THICK

FRONT

GRAIN

ATTACH STAR

GRAIN

SCIPA ©

BACK

GRAIN

GRAIN

scipa ©

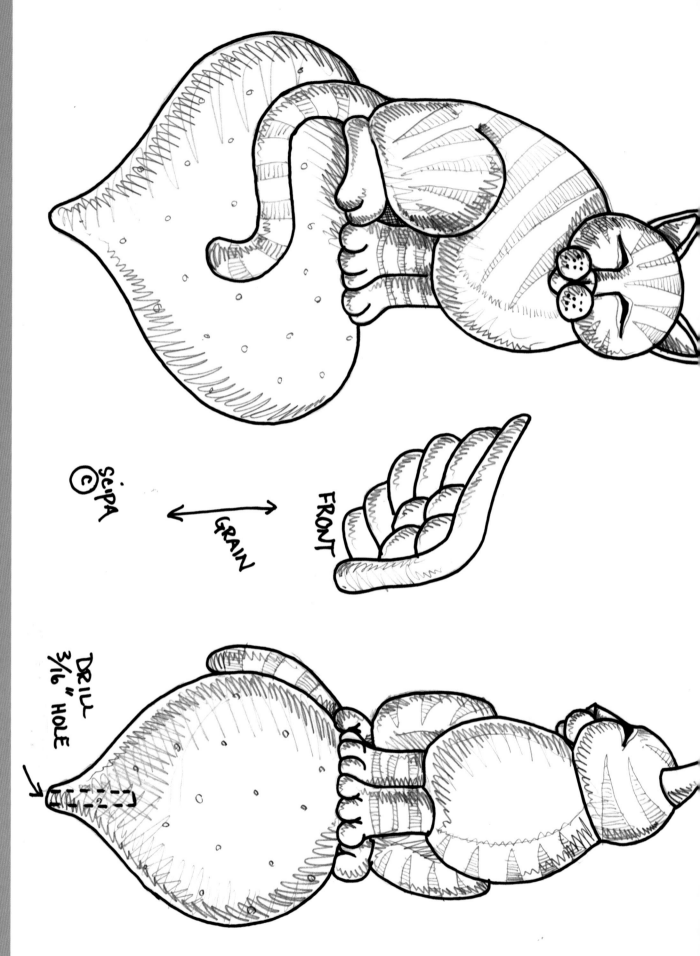

GRAIN

SCIPA ©

FRONT

DRILL 3/16" HOLE

Carving Folk Art Figures • Cupid Cat (1 of 2)

Cupid Cat

This design was originally created as a Valentine's Day gift for my wife, Joanne. At the time, we had a very large orange cat named Tom, who inspired me to carve this. This carving takes some perseverance because all four views are completely different from each other. Despite this, the entire piece can easily be carved with just a knife. The wings are attached in the same manner as the angels' wings. You will notice that I have mounted the carving on a block. I drilled a $^3/_{16}$-inch hole up through the bottom tip of the heart. I then drilled a hole in the center of the block. Last, I drove a large nail up from the bottom into both pieces, securing them with glue. The block measures 4" x 7" x 3". The wings are cut from $^3/_8$-inch-thick stock. If you have a family cat, I'm sure he or she wouldn't mind modeling for you.

Pattern on pages 72 and 74.

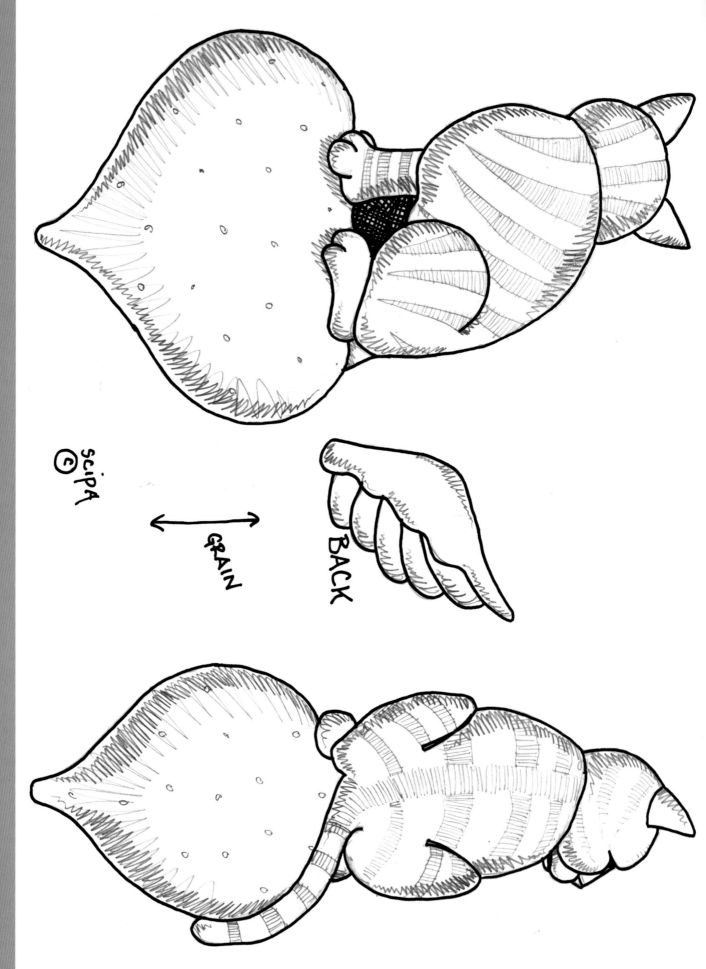

©
scipa

GRAIN

BACK

About the Author

Shawn Cipa began carving in 1993 after his wife, Joanne, bought him a small set of palm tools for Christmas.

Because Shawn possessed a solid background in art, it wasn't long before woodcarving became a driving passion in his life. He began by carving wood spirits. Soon after, he tried his hand at carving Old Father Christmas. Although Shawn has carved many different subjects by commission, he admittedly prefers all things whimsical in nature. Walking sticks, canes, Santas, angels and other mythical characters are just some of Shawn's repertoire.

Shawn comes from an artistic family and has experience in several art forms, such as illustration, painting and sculpture. His mother, a free thinker, and his father, a successful graphic designer of several decades, provided the creative atmosphere necessary to spur him on and develop his skills. Although most art mediums came easily to Shawn, carving wasn't one of them. It was a daunting task to learn to sculpt by *taking away*, rather than adding on, such as in clay sculpturing. However, perseverance has paid off. Other skills include carpentry, photography and amateur astronomy. Shawn is also an accomplished musician of many years, a passion rivaling his love of the visual arts.

Shawn was recently recognized as a national winner in Woodcraft Supply Corporation's first annual Santa carving contest. This accomplishment has helped him earn a name in the woodcarving community and opened the door for the creation of his first book. Shawn hopes to continue his carving endeavors with unending support from his wife, Joanne, as well as his family and friends, who have helped to encourage him on.

Please feel free to contact Shawn by visiting his Website at: *www.shawnscarvings.com.*